BELONGING

KAROLINE M. LEWIS

BELONGING

Five Keys to Unlock
Your Potential as a Disciple

Abingdon Press
Nashville

Belonging:
Five Keys to Unlock Your Potential as a Disciple

Copyright © 2022 Abingdon Press

Library of Congress Control Number: 2022951353

ISBN: 978-1-7910-2583-0

Scripture quotations unless noted otherwise are from the Common English Bible. Copyright © 2011 by the Common English Bible. All rights reserved. Used by permission. www.CommonEnglishBible.com.

Scripture quotations marked KJV are taken from The Authorized (King James) Version. Rights in the Authorized Version in the United Kingdom are vested in the Crown. Reproduced by permission of the Crown's patentee, Cambridge University Press.

Scripture quotations marked NRSVue are taken from the New Revised Standard Version Updated Edition. Copyright © 2021 National Council of Churches of Christ in the United States of America. Used by permission. All rights reserved worldwide.

Scripture quotations marked The Message are taken from THE MESSAGE, copyright © 1993, 1994, 1995, 1996, 2000, 2001, 2002 by Eugene H. Peterson. Used by permission of NavPress. All rights reserved. Represented by Tyndale House Publishers, Inc.

MANUFACTURED IN THE UNITED STATES OF AMERICA

For all who need to leave their water jug behind

Contents

Contents

Prologue

What if every day is the perfect day to finally be exactly who you were always meant to be?

—Tyler Knott Gregson

The woman at the well is my person—that is, my person in the Bible. She can't be my "go-to" person, I guess, given the fact that two thousand years separate us. But almost every day, she inspires me. From her I have learned more about faith, more about myself, and more about God, than from many of my contemporary acquaintances. I admire her. I respect her—this woman with no name who holds her own in a conversation with Jesus and ends up being the first witness to the grace upon grace (John 1:16) that is ours because of Jesus.

I think we all need a person in the Bible, that character who embodies for us what believing in God looks like and feels like. In them we see aspects of ourselves. It is through them that we are better able to articulate what faith means in our own lives. It is through them that we gain a better sense of who God is calling us to be. In them we also see who God is and key characteristics of God, because God made God's very self known to them. God showed up in their lives, and they responded in ways with which we resonate.

Consider who this person in the Bible might be for you. What is it about this character that rings true to you, in whom you see attributes of yourself, your own discipleship self? Maybe you can even imagine being friends. Sitting down for a cup of coffee or going out to lunch. Maybe it's the biblical person you most want to meet in heaven. What about God has this person taught you or that you have always thought to be true about God, that you have hoped about God? What has this character showed you about God that still remains important for you today?

This book invites you on an exploration of one character in Scripture toward discovery of your biblical person—and hopefully, of yourself as a person of faith, maybe even learning a little more about God in the process. How we understand discipleship, faith in Jesus, and the Christian life is not just based on church tradition or denominational instruction but is also a very personal construction. Somewhere in the history of our developing belief in and relationship with Jesus, we likely latched on to a story in the Bible in which we could see ourselves. The story helped us make sense of our own experiences of God. We connected with the characters, the scene, the details, the conversation—and with what the story revealed about God. Perhaps without realizing it at the time, the story shaped both our life with Jesus and our knowing of God.

We have a tendency to put discipleship in a one-size-fits-all category—that there are certain expectations or requirements for how to live as a Christian that we must follow, especially if we want a life with Jesus beyond the grave. Our inclinations toward competition in faith or absolutism about belief have us convinced that there has to be only one way to follow Jesus, that we need to get this discipleship thing "right" so as to secure a mansion (or at least a few comfortable rooms!) in heaven. Yet, a skimming of the Gospels shows us that the disciples were not a uniform bunch. Comparison among Matthew, Mark, Luke, and John confirms that these four evangelists—these writers of the Gospels—present very different portraits of discipleship. Based on their primary christological viewpoint—that is, their essential understanding of Jesus's ministry—Matthew, Mark, Luke, and John offer four unique perspectives of what discipleship looks like. That could make us nervous—shouldn't they have gotten their stories straight? But if that was the goal of the Gospel writers, where would that leave us? What about our relationships with Jesus? Don't they count? I think they do, and that's one of the reasons I love the Samaritan woman at the well. Her story reminds me that my story matters. After all, the woman at the well is not an "official disciple." She's not included on any of Jesus's lists. She doesn't have all the answers. She doesn't even go looking for Jesus; Jesus goes looking for her.

The woman at the well shows us that being a disciple of Jesus is not limited to those twelve named—isn't that a relief?—and the Gospels writers couldn't even agree on the names of the twelve (Matthew 10:2-4; Mark 3:13-19; Luke 6:12-16; see also Acts 1:13-14). Jesus collects followers as he goes along, and often the most unlikely and unexpected individuals. Some have names, like Mary and Martha (John 11–12:8; Luke 10:38-42), Zacchaeus (Luke 19:1-9), or Joseph of Arimathea (John 19:38-42), but most of them don't—like the man born blind who was healed (John 9:1-41) or the women who had been cured of evil spirits and infirmities (Luke 8:1-3). I hope you find a sense of comfort—maybe even a sense of awe—in the fact that Jesus invites people to follow him somewhat indiscriminately. We are also members of the most surprising cast of characters to take up the cross and follow Jesus. We are the Gentiles, after all. We are the outsiders, objects of God's love that those first twelve disciples could never have imagined, just like the Samaritan woman at the well. Jesus sends those first followers out into the world because God loves the world, and look what happened. It seems Jesus meant it when he said, "God so loved the world" (John 3:16).

Even beyond the four Gospels, the rest of the New Testament tells stories of all kinds of different Christian communities trying their best to live Christian lives. From the early churches to which Paul writes, to the seven churches who received the book of Revelation, these groups of believers had to figure out what believing in Jesus looked like in their own contexts and with different challenges, both within their communities and from without. It wasn't easy being a Christian then, and many days, it's not easy being a Christian now. It is important to remember that the first followers of Jesus were not Christian at all—and neither was Jesus. Jesus was a Jew, and the first disciples were Jewish. The Jesus movement, we might call it, was an offshoot of Judaism made up of people who believed that Jesus was the expected Messiah. The writings of the New Testament don't tell us what we *have* to do as disciples but invite us to discuss and imagine how discipleship plays out in the real lives of the followers of Jesus—including us.

In the woman at the well, we discover what discipleship looks like embodied in a particular individual whose life is changed by her encounter with Jesus. Her encounter with Jesus unlocks her potential as a disciple of Jesus and offers us five keys for what belonging to Jesus means: *discomfort, wonder, trust, letting go, witness*. By overhearing her conversation with Jesus, perhaps we can better imagine how our own discipleship has come about and better appreciate how we live it out. This encounter at Jacob's well should feel encouraging—that your own faith experiences can be trusted. That your own encounters with Jesus are worthy of reflection. And that you, as a disciple of Jesus, matter to Jesus—and to God.

This book is divided into five chapters for individual devotional or group study. The five chapters move through the five sections of the conversation, as each section opens up one of the five keys to unlock your potential as a disciple of Jesus. After a general *Introduction* to the Gospel of John with background information that will help us with our study of John 4:1-42, the five main chapters focus on a portion of the dialogue between Jesus and the woman at the well. Each chapter opens with *Focus Verses* and then provides additional passages in the Gospel of John that will be helpful background reading to understand what's going on in John 4 (*Read*). Next is an overview of the specific section of the conversation, highlighting important issues and themes that connect to other parts of the Fourth Gospel (*Review*). Points for discussion follow (*Reflect*), each point followed by topics and questions for further consideration or conversation (*Respond*). The chapters close with a summary of the discipleship key that we have learned from the woman at the well (*Renew*) and then end with *Prayer*. There is also some space at the end of each chapter for you to take notes (*Notes to Self*). The *Epilogue* concludes the book.

The Samaritan woman at the well merits my words of gratitude. Her wonder and trust, her courage and witness continue to inspire me when my faith wanders and assure me when my faith wanes. I am humbled and honored to have given her story the attention it deserves. I am so very thankful to Constance Stella, my editor at Abingdon Press, who has now shepherded three "Five Keys" books. Thank you, Connie, for your support and belief in me. As the woman at the well is my biblical person, I have my persons now whom I admire and who help me be a better disciple of Jesus. They have accompanied me with such grace and love in bringing the Samaritan woman's witness to life. Thank you, Gwen Fulsang, Sarah Anderson, Lisa Bass, Lisa Cressman, Shannyn Fuerst, Terri Delebo, and the Gift Squad for being my women at the well today.

I pray that in listening to this extraordinary conversation between Jesus and the woman at the well, you will be able to hear how God is calling you to your own life of discipleship. This holy calling is not about having all the answers but leaning into the questions by which you might discover who God has called you to be—for the sake of the world God loves so much. Jesus doesn't ask us to get it right, but to be in relationship—with him and with others. In the end, what I hope you will discover is that discipleship is not so much about doing but belonging.

Karoline M. Lewis
Pentecost 2022

Introduction

There are two ways of spreading light—to be the candle
or the mirror that reflects it.

—Edith Wharton

We are about to overhear a conversation between Jesus and the Samaritan woman at the well; it is a conversation that changed her life and changed the lives of the disciples as well. But before we sit down and listen to this dialogue, a few words by way of introduction. This book is not a study of the Gospel of John per se, but it is good to have a little bit of background about this Gospel since the story of the Samaritan woman at the well is unique to the Fourth Gospel. Having an overall sense of what John's Gospel is like will assist us in our understanding of this story. We will be reading around a lot in the Gospel because of the many connections between John 4:1-42 and the rest of the narrative. The whole of the Gospel of John, as well as what we can know about John's audience and purpose for writing, informs our study of the woman at the well and makes for a much richer reading.

Background

The Gospel of John is frequently called "The Fourth Gospel" because it is fourth in the New Testament. If you have ever read the Gospel of

John, compared to the first three Gospels, you probably felt like you had dropped down into an alternative universe. There are many similarities among Matthew, Mark, and Luke, but John feels like that fourth cousin, twice removed. Matthew, Mark, and Luke are often referred to as the "Synoptic Gospels." *Synoptic* is a Greek word that means "see with" or "see together." *Syn* is "with" or "together" in Greek and *optic*, like in English, is the root "to see." *Synoptic* is a term adopted for Matthew, Mark, and Luke because of the parallels among the three. Scholarly consensus these days is that Mark was the first Gospel written, sometime between 70 and 75 CE (*Common Era*; or AD, *Anno Domini*, Latin for "in the year of the Lord") or immediately after the fall of Jerusalem and the Jewish temple to the Romans in 70 CE. Mark's Gospel includes stories and teachings of Jesus passed down through oral tradition between the death and resurrection of Jesus and the collapse of Jerusalem. Around 75 to 85 CE, Matthew and Luke were written, following closely Mark's outline, but also having their own exclusive sources that explain the material that is unique to them respectively, called "M" for Matthew's distinctive source and "L" for Luke's. Scholars also posit that Matthew and Luke had access to another source, designated "Q" from the German word *quelle*, which means "source." This is a hypothetical source—there is no actual existing manuscript in our possession—that includes the sayings of Jesus collected over the years that are found in both Matthew and Luke.

For a number of years, the Gospel of John was dated much later than Matthew and Luke, close to the end of the first century CE, assuming that John's portrait of Jesus, often described as a "high Christology," would need decades to develop. The description "high Christology" typically means that John's portrait of Jesus emphasizes Jesus's divinity more than Matthew, Mark, and Luke, which focus more on Jesus's human traits. Most scholars now date John around the same time as Matthew and Luke, supposing that John simply had different sources available. The discovery of the Dead Sea Scrolls (1947/48) was instrumental in this conclusion, in that the writings of the Jewish community unearthed at Qumran have similar themes and terminology to that found in John. There is a lot of debate about whether or not John knew of the Synoptic tradition, but at the end of the day, we will never know. Some of the most familiar stories of the Bible are only found in John: the wedding at Cana; the character Nicodemus; the raising of Lazarus from the dead; Jesus washing the disciples' feet; and doubting Thomas. Like that of Matthew, Mark, and Luke, the authorship of John is unknown. Early on, tradition "assigned" authorship of the Gospels to the first apostles to establish their authority as writings of the church.

Maybe a more fruitful question to ask is, to whom was this Gospel written? Knowing something about the community helps us make better sense of what John is talking about and why the Fourth Evangelist focuses on some issues and not others. Remember in the *Prologue*, it was noted that the early followers of Jesus were a group of believers from within Judaism. The general proposal is that John was written to a Jewish community that had been expelled from its local synagogue for claiming that Jesus was the Messiah. This is why, in part, John's Gospel sounds very either/or, setting up oppositions and dualities. You are either in or out, either in the light or in the darkness. It has a kind of sectarian ring to it—like a fringe group of people trying to affirm what it believes. Knowing the situation of the community is also important to prevent misreadings of John. For many years, John has been a primary biblical resource to validate anti-Semitism, which is hostility to or prejudice against Jewish people. And yet, Jesus was a Jew. John is best understood as representing an intra-Jewish debate. There was not one monolithic or uniform understanding of Judaism at the time of Jesus. So, Jesus's ministry, along with his followers, was a movement within Judaism. We might make a comparison to Christianity these days. There is not just one way to be a Christian. We have various Christian expressions—think of all the different denominations out there such as Roman Catholic, Methodist, Episcopal, Lutheran, Baptist, Moravian, Presbyterian, Pentecostal—each one having different beliefs. No one denomination has a hold on what it means to be

Christian, although they might like to! In the Gospel of John, when Jesus, who is perceived as someone with religious authority like the Pharisees or Sadducees, has disagreements, they are conflicts with other recognized Jewish religious leaders. As a result, almost every time (depending on the context, of course) you see "the Jews" in the Gospel of John, insert "Jewish leaders" or "Jewish authorities." The Jewish authorities aren't bad people. Rather, their quarrels with Jesus reflect the Jewish religious dialogue that was happening at the time of Jesus.

It is helpful to have an overall sense of the outline of the Gospel of John and some of the Gospel's themes. I am always more interested in paying attention to the text we have in front of us rather than how it got there. There is only so much we can know behind the text, so let's get to know better the story passed down to us. The outline for the Fourth Gospel is pretty straightforward. John can be divided into two major sections: chapters 1–12 are often called the "Book of Signs" because they recount Jesus's three-year ministry, particularly the seven miracles, or signs, Jesus performs along the way. These signs are never called miracles, but "signs" because they point to something beyond the miracle itself that we need to realize about Jesus. Whereas in Matthew, Mark, and Luke, Jesus's ministry takes place over the course of a year and all in the region of Galilee, in John, Jesus is back and forth between Galilee and Jerusalem. You might want to take a look at a map of Palestine at the time of Jesus's ministry to familiarize yourself with the region. Galilee is in the northern part and Jerusalem in the southern part. In John, Jesus travels to Jerusalem for the Jewish pilgrimage feasts. A devout Jewish male was required to go to the Jewish temple in Jerusalem for the three pilgrimage festivals—Weeks, Booths or Tabernacles, and Passover. In John, Jesus is in Jerusalem for the Festival of Booths (chapters 7–8) and for Passover three times (John 2:13; 6:4; 11:55; 12:1; 13:1). It is from John's Gospel that we get a three-year ministry for Jesus because of the three separate references to Jesus being in Jerusalem for Passover. Jesus is also in Jerusalem for the Feast of Dedication (Hanukkah) in chapter 10 (verse 22) and for an unnamed festival in chapter 5 (verse1). Chapters 13–21 are referred to as the "Book of Glory." These chapters narrate the events of the foot washing and Jesus's last meal with his disciples, his arrest, trial, crucifixion, burial, and resurrection appearances, all taking place a little over a week or so.

The first eighteen verses of John are called the Prologue (John 1:1-18) because they introduce the major themes of the Gospel and are set off from the start of Jesus's public ministry. The rest of the narrative can be outlined like this:

The Calling of the Disciples (1:19-51)

The First Sign and the Temple Incident (2)

Tale of Two Disciples: Nicodemus and the Samaritan Woman at the
　　Well (3–4)

Signs and Wonders (5)

The Bread of Life (6)

Conflict (7–8)

The Blind Man, the Door, and the Shepherd (9–10)

The Last Sign—the Raising of Lazarus (11)

Anointing and Arrival in Jerusalem (12)

The Farewell Discourse (13–17)

The Passion Narrative (18–19)

Resurrection Appearances (20–21)

Having a sense of where the conversation between Jesus and the Samaritan woman is located in the overall outline of the Gospel is crucial. We see that this encounter at the well takes place very early on in Jesus's ministry. Jesus has called his first disciples (John 1:35-51). Jesus has been in Cana, the scene for his first sign, saving a wedding reception by turning water into wine. Jesus has journeyed to Jerusalem for Passover where the temple incident occurs (John 2:13-25), which in the Synoptic Gospels is at the end of Jesus's ministry (Matthew 21:12-17; Mark 11:15-19; Luke 19:45-48)—more about that later. The nighttime encounter with Nicodemus immediately precedes the meeting of Jesus and the woman at the well. All these incidents leave us with questions as we travel with Jesus and his disciples from Jerusalem, through Samaria, and up to Galilee: Will there be more disciples called on their journey? Will there be another miracle in Samaria? Will there be another surprise inquirer, like Nicodemus?

Themes in John

Several prominent themes reoccur throughout the narrative in the Gospel of John. We will look at five themes that are helpful to have in mind as we listen in on the conversation between Jesus and the woman at the well. These themes will help us make connections between John 4 and other parts of the Gospel. When we focus just on one story or passage in the Bible, which is usually the case for sermons, we tend to forget that they are part of a larger narrative. How the whole of the story helps us interpret a part is essential for the faithful reading of Scripture—or any book, for that matter. It's hard to follow a murder mystery novel, for example, without following the clues dropped along the way.

The first theme that will assist in our reading of John 4 is rebirth/new creation, set out in the opening phrase of the Prologue, "In the beginning." These are the very same words that open the book of Genesis in the Greek translation of the Old Testament, which is called the Septuagint. When the Gospels were written, few people, if any, read or spoke Hebrew, so the writers of the New Testament relied on their Scriptures (what we call the Old Testament) having been translated into Greek. At the time of Jesus, Palestine was a province of the Roman Empire, which meant Greek was the language of the day. By quoting the first words of the book of Genesis, John makes a connection back to the creation story. This theme of creation becomes important for understanding what Jesus's ministry means. Through the Word that was from God and with God (John 1:1) coming into the world, we can be born anew as children of God:

> But those who did welcome him,
> those who believed in his name,
> he authorized to become God's children,
> born not from blood
> nor from human desire or passion,
> but born from God. (John 1:12-13)

Everything is created through Jesus, and nothing came into being without him. Life is possible because of Jesus (John 1:3-4)! Jesus will offer this new life to Nicodemus: Jesus answered, "I assure you, unless someone is born anew, it's not possible to see God's kingdom" (John 3:3). Then Jesus goes on to say, "I assure you, unless someone is born of water and the Spirit, it's not possible to enter God's kingdom" (John 3:5). Being born anew is possible because of the gift of the Holy Spirit. When Jesus finds the disciples hiding out behind locked doors, he gives them the Holy Spirit promised to them in the Farewell Discourse (John 14:8-17, 25-27; 15:26-27; 16:4b-11). While most English translations read "he breathed on them," the verb here (*emphysaō*, where we get the word *emphysema*) should be translated "breathed into them." It's the same verb used in the Septuagint in Genesis 2:7: "the LORD God formed the human from the topsoil of the fertile land and blew life's breath into his nostrils. The human came to life." And it's the same verb used in Ezekiel 37:9, "He said to me, 'Prophesy to the breath; prophesy, human one! Say to the breath, The Lord God proclaims: Come from the four winds, breath! Breathe into these dead bodies and let them live.'" With God's very breath (the word *pneuma* in Greek can be translated "spirit," "wind," and "breath") we are reborn children of God (John 1:12-13), and it will be God's breath that nourishes us. In belonging, one is born anew, again, from above. How will the woman at the well be born anew?

The second theme to pay attention to is Jesus's identity. John is the clearest of all the Gospel writers that Jesus is God begotten, the one and only God (John 1:18). The Word was, in the beginning, with God and the Word became flesh (John 1:14), the very presence of the one and only God in our midst, the great "I AM" (John 4:26; 6:20; 8:24, 28, 58; 13:19; 18:5, 7). Nicodemus does not recognize who Jesus is. Will the woman at the well see that in Jesus, God is revealing God's very self? Related to Jesus's identity is the identity of those who follow Jesus; they are cast as believers, disciples, sheep in Jesus's fold (10:1-10), those who are "in the light." Thus, the metaphor of light/darkness in the Gospel of John communicates one's relationship, or lack thereof, with Jesus/God. If one is in the light, one is a believer, in a relationship with Jesus. If someone is in the dark/night, they are not in a relationship with Jesus or have rejected a relationship with Jesus. This metaphor is set out in the Prologue, "Through the Word was life, / and the life was the light for all people. / The light shines in the darkness, / and the darkness doesn't extinguish the light" (John 1:4-5). In the rest of the Gospel of John, references to the time of day are much more than details of happenstance. They indicate the status of a person's relationship with Jesus. Nicodemus comes to Jesus "at night;" the woman at the well meets Jesus when it was "about noon." How the Fourth Gospel works out the concept of judgment is then related to the metaphor of light/darkness. John is clear that Jesus was not sent to condemn the world or judge the world, "God didn't send his Son into the world to judge the world, but that the world might be saved through him" (John 3:17). At the same time, judgment happens because people choose darkness rather than the light, "This is the basis for judgment: The light came into the world, and people loved darkness more than the light, for their actions are evil" (John 3:19). In other words, John is saying that we actually judge ourselves based on our response to Jesus. The word *judgment* in Greek is *krisis* and it's where we get the word *crisis*. One's encounter with Jesus, the revelation of God, is a crisis moment, a moment of decision and response, and determines one's relationship with Jesus going forward. Will the Samaritan woman see Jesus's true identity? Will she end up in the darkness or in the light?

The third theme is relationship. Just as Jesus and God have an intimate relationship from the beginning, "the Word was *with* God" (John 1:1 my emphasis) and as Father and Son (John 1:18), believers are brought into this relationship as well. The whole point of the Word becoming flesh is for God to love the world, for the believer to experience the love and union that the Father and Son share. But this isn't just any kind of relationship— it is very intimate, a kind of closeness that might take us by surprise. In the Prologue, we discover just how close this relationship is, "No one has ever seen God. / God the only Son, / who is at the Father's side, / has made God known" (John 1:18). While most of our Bibles will say "at the Father's side" or "close to the Father's heart," the word translated as "side" or "heart" is really "bosom" or "breast." The only other time this word is used in the Gospel of John is when the Beloved Disciple, the disciple whom Jesus loved, is introduced for the first time in the story, "One of the disciples, the one whom Jesus loved, was at Jesus's side" (John 13:23), where, again, "side" is "breast." Jesus invites all to share in this intimate, tender, loving, nurturing, sustaining relationship with him and with God. It is a relationship that leads to abundant life (John 10:10) and eternal life (John 17:3). In fact, for John, this relationship, we shall see, *is* eternal life. Our home with God is not only promised to us in the resurrection—"My Father's house has room to spare. If that weren't the case, would I have told you that I'm going to prepare a place for you?" (John 14:2)—but is present for us here and now. As a result, the concept of "sin" has a very distinctive meaning in John. "Sin" is therefore not a moral category but is the rejection of the relationship that Jesus offers. When John the Baptist cries, "Look! The Lamb of God who takes away the sin of the world!" (John 1:29), it means that in the coming of Jesus, our separation from God is no longer. A relationship with God has been restored or made possible in the life, death, resurrection, and ascension of Jesus. In reading

John 4, what will a relationship with Jesus make possible for the woman at the well? What will abundant life mean for her?

The fourth theme, important for interpreting the story of the woman at the well, is witness, which, besides relationship, is the primary description of discipleship in the Gospel of John. It is our last key for unlocking your potential as a disciple. Even John the Baptist in the Gospel of John is portrayed primarily as a witness to Jesus, not as the one who baptizes him, "A man named John was sent from God. He came as a witness to testify concerning the light, so that through him everyone would believe in the light. He himself wasn't the light, but his mission was to testify concerning the light" (John 1:6-8; also read the account of Jesus's baptism in John 1:29-34). To witness or to testify (it's the same word in Greek) to Jesus is to point to his presence in our midst and to invite people to their own encounter with Jesus. Discipleship can take on many different expressions! For example, Matthew presents the disciples primarily as pupils of a rabbi, students of the great teacher, Jesus. In John, what does witnessing look like? Encountering the woman at the well, we will want to ask, how is she a witness?

A last theme to listen for in our study of the woman at the well is abundance: "I came so that they could have life—indeed, so that they could live life to the fullest" (John 10:10). This abundance again comes from the Prologue, "From his fullness we have all received grace upon grace" (John 1:16). After 1:17, the word grace never again appears in the Gospel of John. Instead, each encounter with Jesus is meant to be an occurrence of grace upon grace. Grace is not definable but can only be experienced. We want to pay attention to the ways in which God's presence in Jesus is a moment of overflowing grace for the woman at the well. How might we articulate what grace means, or define grace, because of her encounter with the living God? These five themes—rebirth/new creation, Jesus's identity, relationship, witness, and abundance—are interwoven within the story of the woman at the well and within the Fourth Gospel.

One final guiding thought before we move specifically to some introductory aspects of John 4:1-42. The Gospels are not simply information about Jesus. They are not neutral documents because there is something at stake—a courageous claim that in Jesus, our God is here. Believing that Jesus is the Messiah, the Son of God, God incarnate in our midst, the Gospel writers want us to believe the same. This means that we cannot be passive in our engagement with these narratives that call themselves the "good news about Jesus Christ" (Mark 1:1). The Fourth Evangelist is clear about the intended goal of the Gospel: "Then Jesus did many other miraculous signs in his disciples' presence, signs that aren't recorded in this scroll. But these things are written so that you will believe that Jesus is the Christ, God's Son, and that believing, you will have life in his name" (John 20:30-31). John narrates this account of Jesus's ministry so that we might believe! For some, this means coming to belief when you have not believed in Jesus before (John 3:16; 10:16); for those already disciples, for you and for me, this means being sustained, supported, and nurtured in your believing as the one whom Jesus loves, because sometimes, having faith is hard work. Read the story of the woman at the well at your own risk. Don't expect to walk away the same person who came to the well at noon on that warm spring day. Something is going to happen to you.

Introduction to John 4:1-42

Before we dive into this incredible conversation, a little background specific to this chapter is necessary. The story is exclusive to John's Gospel, appearing nowhere else in Scripture. When that happens, we want to ask, what about this story is especially "Johannine" (having to do with John) in nature? We would ask the same question for unique stories to Matthew, Mark, or Luke. For example, why is the story of the prodigal son only in Luke? How does it communicate themes that are specific to Luke's portrait of Jesus? Comparing the Gospels yields important differences in how each writer conceived of the meaning and purpose of Jesus's ministry.

Remember that when the New Testament was being put together, we could have had only one Gospel, likely Matthew because the early church took a liking to Matthew, and for many years, it was thought to be the first Gospel written. Another popular Gospel-like document floating around in the early years of Christianity was Tatian's *Diatesseron* (circa 150 CE). Tatian was an Assyrian apologist, a student of the early church father Justin Martyr, who created a harmonized version of Matthew, Mark, Luke, and John. It was very popular. When it came time to canonize the New Testament, Matthew, Mark, Luke, and John were included on their own merits, the church thereby celebrating the particularity of each Gospel. The New Testament is a collection of twenty-seven books, with each writer trying to express a certain conviction about the person and work of Christ. It is quite a diverse library! As persons of faith who draw on the New Testament for understanding God and God's activity in Jesus, we read thoughtfully and listen carefully for God's special Word for us in that moment and in that biblical passage. Paying careful attention to the variety of voices in Scripture can feel like swimming upstream, when most often we hear the phrase, "the Bible says." But, a disregard for the unique voice of each biblical writing dishonors that author's attempt to understand how God is at work in the world. When we feel the pull of the undertow of blended testimony or harmonization, we might ask— would we want our own individual witness to get lost in the whirlpool of opinions?

Another feature of this story to observe on the front end is the obvious comparison between the conversation Jesus has with Nicodemus in the chapter just before (John 3:1-21) and the conversation Jesus has with the Samaritan woman at the well. It is not accidental that these two conversations are placed side-by-side in the narrative. The divergences are striking: Nicodemus is a male, he has a name, and he is a religious leader; the conversation between him and Jesus takes place in Jerusalem (the religious center of Judaism) during Passover; Nicodemus approaches Jesus by night, "Nick at night" I like to call him, he misunderstands what

Jesus is offering him, and the short conversation ends with Nicodemus being a little on the clueless side: "How can these things be?" (John 3:9). By contrast, the woman at the well is female, she does not have a name, and she is a religious outsider; the conversation between her and Jesus takes place in Sychar, Samaria, an area where no Jew would travel; the conversation takes place at noon, the brightest time of the day; while she initially misunderstands Jesus, she is more open to what he has to say and what he offers, thereby moving much further along in the conversation compared to Nicodemus, and she ends up being a witness for Jesus to her whole town. In the comparison is meaning, and we as readers are asked to imagine how we would do in a conversation with Jesus.

If your church uses the Revised Common Lectionary, a listing of texts within a three-year cycle used by such denominations as Lutheran, Episcopalian, Methodist, United Church of Christ, and Presbyterian, this passage appears in Year A, the year that focuses on the Gospel of Matthew. John 4:5-42 is the Gospel reading for the third Sunday of Lent. In fact, it is the second of four readings in a row from the Gospel of John in Year A: John 3:1-21 (Jesus's encounter with Nicodemus), John 4:1-42, John 9:1-41 (the healing of the man born blind), and John 11:1-45 (the raising of Lazarus from the dead). Can you remember any sermons on the Samaritan woman at the well and what the main points were? What are some of your assumptions about this passage that might be based on sermons you have heard? What lingering questions have you had about this meeting at the well? Our reading of the Bible is always shaped by what we have already read or heard or been taught about it. Just because someone preached a sermon or wrote an essay on John 4 does not make that person's interpretation authoritative—or even correct. We all come to Scripture with our own biases. We read from the intersection of the many contexts that have shaped who we are, such as gender, demographics, family relationships, education, religious history, and our own individual experiences. We hear what we want to hear. We listen for what we think we already know. A deep dive into one passage, one story in the Bible, invites the possibility of slowing down, taking our time, really sitting in and with the story, being open to discovering something new—about the story, about the characters, about God, about ourselves.

John 4:1-42 narrates the longest conversation between Jesus and a character in all of the Gospels. Given this observation, we can make several important conclusions. First, that is a lot of narrative space given to a conversation, especially between Jesus and an assumed outsider or marginalized person. That much space indicates importance, that we should pay close attention to this dialogue, what gets said and what doesn't. This is not a brief, secondary exchange, but a highlighted meeting of opposites and enemies into which we are drawn. Second, it communicates that conversation is important for a life of faith. We gather together around the Bible, we come together in various church and community settings, eager for dialogue, with a spirit of curiosity and wonder. Do we want answers or to engage in conversation around what we believe, to ask questions, and to listen to and learn from others. Conversation is essential for an active and living faith. Third, it means that what is being told in this story cannot easily be distilled into a pithy phrase, a clear doctrine, a moral for the ages, or a plaque for our walls. Faith and relationship take time. We might think of faith, then, not as something we have, but as a way of living, a way of being in the world. The narrative space given to this conversation suggests that the focus of this story is the relationship that the woman at the well and Jesus begin; a relationship that will continue beyond the story and beyond the last words of the Gospel. Faith in Jesus is an ongoing relationship, not something you obtain or that can be summarized or contained in one simple statement. Faith is an invitation to life-long conversation with Jesus.

Reflect and Respond

- Read the Gospel of John in its entirety to prepare for the study that follows. Make notes on where in the whole of the Gospel you see the themes outlined above. What connections are you starting to make between John 4:1-42 and other parts of John's Gospel? Where do you see the themes presented above "in action"? How are these correlations shaping your reading of John 4:1-42 so far?

- Reread John 4:1-42 on its own. Where do you see some of these themes playing out? Now, listen to John 4:1-42. This is another way to experience biblical stories/passages, especially how they would have been encountered in the earlier days. The writings of the Bible were meant to be heard and not read. Oral communication was the primary form of media until the invention of the printing press (by Johannes Gutenberg in 1450), which enabled distribution of information and material in printed form. Before the first translations of the Bible into the language of the people (late fifteenth century), nobody could read the Bible. Sometimes when we read, we do so quickly, thinking that we know how the story goes. Listening to biblical passage forces us to slow down. Take notes along the way. What do you hear that you did not read?

- Have you ever thought about who's your favorite person in the Bible and why? What has that person taught you about God? About Jesus? About yourself?

- What characteristics have you usually associated with discipleship? Where did they come from? Have you ever felt like your discipleship did not measure up in some way? Why or why not? How do you describe yourself when you think of discipleship or of being a believer?

Get ready! We are about to overhear a conversation that changed the life of an unnamed woman at a well, a woman just minding her own business, doing what she had to do. Don't be surprised if your life is changed as well.

Prayer

Loving God, thank you for speaking through John to share a story of your Son. Help us to hear in this story of the woman at the well our own story of our relationship with you and with your Son, Jesus. Guide us, in love, in grace, into your truth—for Jesus is the Truth.

Notes to Self

_____

_____

_____

_____

_____

_____

_____

_____

_____

_____

_____

_____

_____

_____

_____

_____

Chapter One

Discomfort

Most of us spend so much time thinking about where we have been or where we are supposed to be going that we have a hard time recognizing where we actually are. When someone asks us where we want to be in our lives, the last thing that occurs to us is to look down at our feet and say, "Here, I guess, since this is where I am."

—Barbara Brown Taylor

Focus Verses: John 4:1-6

¹Jesus learned that the Pharisees had heard that he was making more disciples and baptizing more than John (²although Jesus' disciples were baptizing, not Jesus himself). ³Therefore, he left Judea and went back to Galilee. ⁴Jesus had to go through Samaria. ⁵He came to a Samaritan city called Sychar, which was near the land Jacob had given to his son Joseph. ⁶Jacob's well was there. Jesus was tired from his journey, so he sat down at the well. It was about noon.

Read

Read the following passages in the Gospel of John. Note how they illustrate the five themes discussed in the *Introduction* (rebirth/new creation; identity of Jesus; relationship; witness; abundance) and the connections you are making to the *Focus Verses*.

John 1:1-5

John 1:35-51

John 3:1-21

John 15:18-27

John 16:1-4

Review

The opening verses of the Samaritan woman's encounter with Jesus at the well set the stage for the conversation. When reading the Bible, you always want to pay attention to the setting—that is, the details that describe where the event is taking place. This information is not accidental but provides background and meaning to the story. What a Bible story might be communicating or what it means in this time and place for you might be found in the smallest of details that establish the setting. Think about when you read a novel; you pay attention to the setting and surroundings because they communicate a great deal about the story, often telling you as much as the plot itself does. Events that occur in our lives are shaped by and remembered for the settings in which we experience them. Events take on particular meaning because of the locations where they happened. The places are part of the experience, part of our meaningful memories. We do not go through our lives simply moving from plot point to plot point, right? Where things happen makes a difference! In the case of John 4:1-6, four specific aspects of the setting are important, for how they create the backdrop for the meeting at the well, how they connect to the overall themes in the Gospel of John, and how they help us make sense of the dialogue that follows.

"he left Judea and went back to Galilee" (4:3)

The first detail to note is where Jesus has been. So far in the story, Jesus has been in Bethany where John was baptizing (John 1:28). Jesus then travels to Galilee, which is the location for the calling of the disciples (John 1:43). In chapter 2, Jesus then heads to Cana, a small town southwest of the Sea of Galilee, to attend a wedding. After the wedding, Jesus and his mother go to Capernaum where they stay for a few days (John 2:12). Then, in John 2:13, Jesus makes his pilgrimage to Jerusalem for Passover. Jesus gets around in John! And places matter. You know what they say: location, location, location! Location does matter. When you are reading the Bible, it's helpful to have access to maps. When reading the New Testament, a map of first-century Palestine is most useful. Biblical geography is sometimes hard to understand because the notations for directions are often different from what we use. For example, when we read in John 2:13 that Jesus "went up" to Jerusalem as it is translated in most Bibles, we might think he went north. But Jesus has been in the northern part of Palestine, in Galilee, and Jerusalem is in the south, in Judea. The direction "up" here indicates that the city of Jerusalem was built on a hill, so one "went up" to Jerusalem. Maybe you have been to Israel/Palestine and can now picture some of these locations in your head. Maybe you remember how meaningful it was to walk in the footsteps of Jesus. Geography then and now is never random but has meaning.

As mentioned in the *Introduction*, in Matthew, Mark, and Luke, Jesus is only in Jerusalem one time during his ministry—his triumphal entry into Jerusalem (Palm Sunday, Matthew 21:12-17; Mark 11:15-19; Luke 19:45-48), after which is the ruckus in the temple and then Jesus's arrest, trial, and crucifixion (the Passion narrative). In John, Jesus journeys to Jerusalem many times during his ministry. Jesus is in Jerusalem for three Passover celebrations over the course of the Gospel, which is his reason for being in Jerusalem at this point in the story. It is in Jerusalem, during Passover, that he meets Nicodemus and now Jesus is traveling back north to Galilee. Recall from our discussion in the *Introduction* that observant male Jews in Palestine were required according to God's law to go to Jerusalem for the three pilgrimage festivals/feasts:

> Three times a year every male among you must appear before the presence of the LORD your God in the location he will select: at the Festival of Unleavened Bread, the Festival of Weeks, and the Festival of Booths. They must not appear before the LORD's presence empty-handed. Each one should have his gift in hand, in precise measure with the blessing the LORD your God gives you. (Deuteronomy 16:16-17)

These festivals remain the primary festival celebrations in modern Judaism. Passover (*Pesah*), or the Feast of Unleavened Bread, is celebrated each year in the spring around the same time as the Christian Easter, commemorating God's deliverance from Egypt and from the plague of the death of the firstborn. The Feast of Weeks (*Pentecost/Shavuot*) is a spring festival marking the first fruits of the wheat harvest, falling fifty days or seven weeks after Passover (the story of Pentecost, meaning "fifty," the coming of the Spirit to the apostles in Acts 2:1-21 falls on Pentecost, "When Pentecost Day arrived, they were all together in one place" [verse 1]). The Feast of Booths or Tabernacles (*Sukkoth*) is a fall festival that marked both the end of the harvest season and the presence of God in the Tabernacle in the wilderness wanderings. In the book of Numbers, after the Exodus from Egypt and before reaching the promised land (the end of the book of Deuteronomy), the Israelites travel for forty years, bringing the ark of the covenant with them, the chest that Moses, while on Mount Sinai, was instructed to build to house the Ten Commandments or the Tablets of Stone (Exodus 25). The Tabernacle was the moveable tent that housed the Ark. It is for this festival that Jesus is in Jerusalem in chapters 7–8 in the Gospel of John.

Having been in Jerusalem for Passover, Jesus is now heading home to Galilee. The distance between Jerusalem and Galilee was about forty miles and would have taken around four days, walking eight to twelve miles a day. We should note here how John takes pains to show that Jesus was an observant male Jew. This is a critical corrective to interpretations of

John that justify anti-Semitism. Jesus is a faithful Jewish male. When Jesus argues with "the Jews" in the Fourth Gospel, it is most of the time Jesus in conversation with other perceived Jewish authorities or Jewish leaders. Jesus presents himself as one with authority to speak about and for God and to interpret the Scriptures—that is, his Scriptures, the Jewish Bible. I suggested in the Introduction that John is best read as capturing an intra-Jewish debate. Jesus is not condemning Jews; that is a misinterpretation of Jesus in John's Gospel. Rather, Jesus is engaged in dialogue, debate, and even conflict with his fellow religious authorities regarding the interpretation of Scripture and his own ministry and identity.

The *Introduction* also discussed how most scholars who study John's Gospel think that John was written to a group within a larger Jewish community whose members had decided to follow Jesus, professing him to be the long-awaited Messiah. Because of this decision, they were then cast out of their community or their synagogue. In the Gospel of John itself, there is textual evidence for this conclusion found in 9:22, 12:42-43, and 16:2 (see also 7:13). In 9:22, the parents of the man born blind are afraid to speak up for their son for fear of being "expelled from the synagogue." In chapter 12, at the end of Jesus's last public discourse before the events of "the hour" begin (John 13:1), there are some authorities who believe in Jesus but fear the same fate as the parents of the man born blind: "Even so, many leaders believed in him, but they wouldn't acknowledge their faith because they feared that the Pharisees would expel them from the synagogue. They believed, but they loved human praise more than God's glory" (John 12:42-43). In the Farewell Discourse, Jesus tells his disciples plainly that they too will be cast out of their communities for their loyalty to Jesus:

> I have said these things to you so that you won't fall away. They will expel you from the synagogue. The time is coming when those who kill you will think that they are doing a service to God. They will do these things because they don't know the Father or me. But I have said these things to you so that when their time comes, you will remember that I told you about them. (John 16:1-4)

"*Jesus had to go through Samaria*" (4:4)

The next detail in these opening verses that we will want to notice is the geographical notation that Jesus had to go through Samaria to travel from Jerusalem to Galilee. Well, no, Jesus didn't. Take a look at your Bible map, sometimes included in the back of our Bibles, or look up online "map of first-century Palestine" and you will see that geographically, Jesus did not have to go through Samaria to get back to Galilee. There were two other possible routes for travel between the northern and southern regions of Palestine: either along the coast of the Mediterranean Sea or along the Jordan River valley. In fact, no Jew would travel through Samaria for fear of coming into contact with a Samaritan. Samaritans live in Samaria!

The Samaritans and the Jews had a complex history marked by animosity. At the time of Jesus, the rift between the Jews and the Samaritans dated back to the split of the northern and southern kingdoms of Israel and the Assyrian conquest of Israel (722 BCE). The Samaritans trace their roots to the Israelites not deported by Assyria, those who stayed behind in the north. The conflict was then fueled by the Babylonian captivity/ exile (586–516 BCE). When the Babylonians destroyed Jerusalem and the temple in 587 BCE, the Jewish people in Israel were forced into Babylon. When the Jews were allowed to return to Judea, they wanted nothing to do with the Samaritans, who had intermingled and intermarried with their Assyrian and Babylonian captors, making the Samaritans unclean. The Jews rebuilt their temple in Jerusalem (the Second Temple), but the Samaritans built their temple on Mount Gerizim (Nablus). While there were many commonalities between the two, by the time of Jesus, the conflict was solidified by the construction of two separate temples for the worship of Yahweh.

Although John tells us that Jesus had to go through Samaria, or, another way to translate the Greek, "it was necessary for him to go through Samaria," this was not geographically true. If it was not a geographical necessity, what then are we to make of this detail? To get the full story, we must go back to the previous chapter, specifically John 3:16: "God so loved the world that he gave his only Son, so that everyone who believes in him won't perish but will have eternal life." When Jesus shares with Nicodemus this truth about his mission and ministry in the world, Jesus is not hoping that his words end up on a poster someday during a football game. Jesus's coming into the world is for the sake of God loving the world. The very purpose of his ministry, the central meaning of the Word becoming flesh, is to bring God's love to the entire world. In fact, the Greek word here is *kosmos*. God truly does love the whole entire world, all of creation, and so in the very next chapter, Jesus takes his disciples through Samaria to show them what the world looks like and who the world is. The world, in this case, is the last person on the planet you would think God could love—a woman, a foreigner, a Samaritan, who has been shunned and shamed for her marital history. Can you imagine what the disciples must have thought? Can you imagine what they must have whispered to each other? I imagine them saying, "Wait, we're going where?" But Jesus needs to show his followers just whom God truly loves—because they will be called to do the same—and the only way to do that was to take them through Samaria to Sychar.

Jesus also goes to Sychar to find a witness, a new disciple. In the calling of the disciples in the Gospel of John (John 1:35-51), the primary metaphor used is that of "finding." Once Andrew follows Jesus, we are then told Andrew first "found" his own brother Simon Peter, saying, "we have found the Messiah" (John 1:41). Jesus then "found" Philip (John 1:43), and Philip "found" Nathanael, saying to him, "We have found the one Moses wrote about in the Law and the Prophets: Jesus, Joseph's son, from Nazareth" (John 1:45). While the actual verb "to find" is not in John 4, we are meant to make a connection back to the calling of the disciples. Jesus travels through Samaria to find this woman at Jacob's well because God loves *the world*! In going to Samaria, Jesus is looking forward to his words in chapter 10, "I have other sheep that don't belong to this sheep pen. I must lead them too. They will listen to my voice and there will be one flock, with one shepherd" (John 10:16). Jesus finding the woman at the well also anticipates the story of the healing of the man born blind in chapter 9. Jesus first finds the man and heals him. The man does not seek out healing from Jesus. Rather, Jesus looks for him, with the possibility of bringing him into the fold of the Good Shepherd (John 10:16). When the formerly blind man is thrown out by the religious leaders for his apparent loyalty to Jesus, Jesus then finds him once again (the same verb used for the calling of the disciples, *heuriskō*, which is where we get the word *eureka*). Jesus has been absent since the healing took place (John 9:7), and yet when he hears that the man he healed has been thrown out (John 9:34), he finds him, (John 9:35), bringing him into the fold of the Good Shepherd. Jesus has to go through Sychar to fulfill John 3:16 and to anticipate his promise in John 10:16. According to the details that the Fourth Evangelist provides, in the woman at the well, Jesus has found yet another disciple. This is her own call to discipleship. This is her call story.

"Jacob's well was there" (4:6)

The third detail to note is the mention of Jacob's well. In addition to being sources of water, wells have an important function in the Old Testament as betrothal scenes. Isaac and Rebekah (Genesis 24:10-27), Jacob and Leah (Genesis 29:1-11), and Moses and Zipporah (Exodus 2:15-22) all met and became engaged to be married at a well. Of course, Jesus does not go to the well to find his future wife! But this backdrop seems important for interpreting this story. First, the well is an intimate place, a place of relationship, promise, and hope. Second, it is a place of provision, especially of water, which we will learn more about in the next part of the conversation. When we discover later on that the woman at the well has had five husbands, who have either divorced her or died on her (we will get to that later), we might wonder, then, how Jesus is now offering her a kind of relationship that she perhaps has never had. Third, the well suggests a commonality, a connection, between the Samaritan woman and Jesus. In fact, the Samaritan woman and Jesus would have had the same ancestry, which she points out later in the conversation (John

4:12). This shared ancestry also implies that indeed, she is part of the world God loves. The well also sets the scene for the conversation about water. She has come there to draw water, a twice-daily job for women in ancient Palestine, but Jesus will offer her living water. And Jesus himself needs water. He is tired from his journey thus far—a reminder that Jesus is human, after all, and he is thirsty. We forget that about Jesus, especially in the Gospel of John where Jesus seems a bit "other-worldly." We are reminded of Jesus's needs, which are the same as hers. Their mutual need brings them to Jacob's well. Notice that John does not set Jesus over and against the woman but places them on a level playing field, perhaps where all good conversations should start.

"it was about noon" (4:6)

Recall that one of the themes of the Gospel of John is the recognition of Jesus as the incarnated Word of God, which gets played out in the metaphor of light and darkness. Light and darkness, then, indicate the status of one's relationship with Jesus. In the Gospel of John, notations about the time of day are never just that alone. They also signify that particular character's recognition of and relationship with Jesus. Jesus is the light of the world, the light that shines in the darkness and the darkness cannot overcome it (John 1:5). If one is in the light, it means that the person has the potential to see the true identity of Jesus as the light of the world. But, if a person is in the dark, they are unable or unwilling to enter into a relationship with Jesus or acknowledge his true identity as the One and Only God (John 1:18).

Remember that Nicodemus comes to Jesus by night (John 3:2). But this conversation in John 4 takes place when the sun is at its highest point in the sky, full and bright. Commentators have offered a number of interpretations for Nicodemus's nighttime rendezvous: he wants to talk to Jesus but does not want his fellow Jewish leaders to know; he's a secret believer; he is fearful of the potential repercussions of talking with Jesus. All suggestions could be possible. However, when we take into account the symbolism of light and darkness in John's Gospel, and that Nicodemus's conversation with Jesus is on the short side—especially compared to the dialogue between Jesus and the woman at the well—that Nicodemus came to Jesus by night might also imply that Nicodemus is not open to a relationship with Jesus. The conversation lasts nine verses before Nicodemus asks, "How can this be?" (John 3:9).

The woman at the well meets Jesus at about noon or, as some translations say, "the sixth hour" as the hours of the day were marked from 6:00 a.m. Noon is the lightest, brightest time of day. When we place Nicodemus and the woman at the well side-by-side, the contrast between these two conversations is even more striking. With this detail of the setting in mind, we might then expect more from the Samaritan woman, and sure enough, her conversation with Jesus lasts much longer, leading her to invite her whole town to come and meet Jesus. She steps into the light, willing and open to imagine what a life with Jesus might look like.

It is essential to point out that this theme of light and darkness in the Gospel of John does not translate into how current society has perpetuated that white is good and black is bad. This is an assumption incorrectly placed on the symbolism of light and darkness in the Gospel of John and comes from a racist bias. We can appreciate this imagery for what it is when we see that John grounds the symbolism of the light and the darkness in the creation story from Genesis. The Gospel begins, "In the beginning," and, as noted in the *Introduction*, the same words are used to open the book of Genesis in the Greek translation of the Old Testament. We are supposed to connect the opening verses of the Gospel of John back to the creation story. It is from God's creation of light in an otherwise dark world that John can say, Jesus is the light of the world. Light shines in the darkness, but light also exposes. Light might not always be considered good if it uncovers truths about ourselves or exposes things we have hidden that we don't want others to see. For example, when Judas leaves the upper room after having his feet washed by Jesus and sharing a meal with his fellow disciples, we are told, "So when Judas took the bread, he left immediately. And it was night" (John 13:30). Cue movie music! Judas's act of betrayal is not when he hands Jesus over with a kiss in the garden (absent in the Gospel of John, see John 18:1-12), but when he abandons his relationship with Jesus, when he rejects the light, or when the light shines the truth on who he truly is. Judas chooses the dark side over the light of the world. This is Judas's crisis moment, his moment of judgment. For the woman at the well, her encounter with the light of the world at noon suggests her openness, her curiosity, and her willingness to remain in the conversation with Jesus, even if it might expose who she truly is. At this point in the story, before the conversation even begins, we should have a greater sense of expectation for her. Given the divergence from Nicodemus, we might be asking, will she fair better than Nicodemus? Will she see what he was unable to see? The conversation continues.

Reflect, Respond, Renew

Reflect

John 3:16 is one of the most well-known verses in Scripture. We find it on plaques, placards, and bumper stickers. Wall art and body art. If anybody's going to know a verse from the Bible, you can pretty much guarantee that verse is John 3:16. But at the same time, it is also one of the most misunderstood, misused, and misinterpreted verses of the Bible. Rather than be a sweeping promise about the inclusiveness of God's love, John 3:16 has been used to exclude and to condemn. It has been used to judge people, to say that if you do not believe in Jesus then you are not saved. We stop at 3:16 when 3:17-21 are quite clear: God did not send God's Son into the world to judge or condemn the world. That's okay, we will! A careful reading of John 3:16 in its context, especially if you keep reading through the first verses of John 4, helps us see John 3:16 for its true meaning. God loves this woman—and fiercely—and so Jesus takes his disciples to Sychar to show them just how huge God's love truly is.

Respond

When, where, and how have you heard John 3:16 being used or quoted? What were the circumstances? What has John 3:16 meant to you in your life of faith? How does your understanding of John 3:16 change given the discussion above? Can you imagine having a conversation with someone about John 3:16 and sharing some of these insights?

Reflect

The idea that God loves the world is not sentimental or emotional. God loving the world is not hypothetical or theoretical. Jesus takes his disciples to Sychar to show them that "God loves the world" is not a fantasy, that God really means it. And loving the world means that God loves the last person on the face of the planet whom we think God could love—a religious outsider, a political complication, a social outcast, a woman, after all. You see, as much as we resist it, God is rather persistent. Jesus intrudes, finding his way into our secluded, safe, and secure spaces. Or, on this side of the COVID-19 pandemic, those quarantine places, those places where we feel the most isolated. When you have been cast out, like the man born blind. When you find yourself all alone at the well, God will find you.

Respond

When you think about God loving the world, what has the world meant to you in the past? Or, what does the world represent? Have you ever thought about the "world" being you? That the one whom God has in mind just might end up being you? Watch out. Jesus just might be on the lookout for you. What will be your response? Do you want to be found? Can you think of a time when Jesus found you, bringing you back to his light? What difference does it make to think of betraying Jesus as leaving or rejecting a relationship with him? Recall your own call story. When did you become a disciple of Jesus? Are there any similarities between your call story and what we have talked about so far about discipleship in the Gospel of John?

Reflect

At the same time that Jesus goes to Sychar to find a witness, to find her, to find you, we can also see ourselves as the disciples in the story. Jesus takes his disciples through Samaria, to Sychar, knowing that they would question the decision. Jesus also knew that the disciples would have to face their discomfort and their fear of coming into contact with Samaritans. Jesus is fully aware that going to Sychar is never easy. We tend to stay clear of difficulty and discomfort and choose expediency. We circumvent the unpleasant and opt for the guarantee. But sometimes God pushes us into places we do not feel ready to go or want to go because we know what might happen in Sychar kinds of places. It's that place, at high noon, that sheds a bright light on our own prejudices, biases, and ideologies. It's that place under that merciless sun that calls attention to all of the –isms from which we thought we were exempt—racism, sexism, ableism. It's that place that calls out our privilege and our suspicions of the other. Sychar exposes our fears of "those people." It tells us the truth about ourselves, truths that we have worked hard to cover up, to deny, and to pretend don't exist. When we read, "he had to go through Samaria," we might truly wish for different.

Respond

The Buddha says, "Three things cannot be long hidden; the SUN, the MOON, and the TRUTH." What truths are you hiding about your life that you find hard even to admit to yourself? If you imagine that light reveals things, what are you afraid might be uncovered about you and about your faith? What are you afraid that others will see? What don't you want Jesus to see? Where and what is your past or present-day Sychar? Where might God be calling you—to which or to whom or to what—that you do not want to go?

Reflect

Going to Sychar also means being vulnerable. It might mean putting yourself in a position of need. A situation of dependence. A circumstance in which you are forced to ask for that which is necessary for your survival, or maybe for that which will cause you to find yourself once again. Sometimes we overlook the fact that Jesus needs something from the woman at the well before she realizes she needs something from Jesus. It's late spring. In Palestine. It's noon. It's warm. And Jesus is tired and thirsty. He needs a drink of water. And she's the only one for miles who has what he needs. Jesus asks her for a drink, placing his need in her hands; and something happens in this exchange that at this moment we can only partially see—where need replaces judgment and love replaces suspicion. A while back I discovered an icon of this story I had never seen before. In it, both Jesus and the woman at the well have halos, signifying holiness. Sacredness. Deification. And both are holding a cup, a chalice, their hands almost touching, where it's impossible to determine who is offering the cup to whom. Nothing has been said in this conversation so far, no words uttered, and yet already we have a sense of mutual dependence, of true reciprocity that is essential for real relationship.

Respond

Why is it so hard to ask for what we need? We pretend to be strong all of the time or try to meet the needs of others before we tend our own. I know I do. But, as the saying goes, we can't help others unless we put on our own oxygen mask first. Have you ever thought that Jesus might need something from you? What might that need be? What does it feel like to be needed by Jesus?

Renew

The setting for the conversation between Jesus and the woman at the well sets up many ways to think about discipleship. But the one I want to emphasize here, Key Number One, is that "going to Sychar" represents discomfort. That is, sometimes our belief in Jesus takes us to places we might not want to go, or even resist. We don't want to be challenged or stretched. We don't want to have our "faith shaken" or have a card pulled out from the proverbial house of cards we have constructed that represents our faith. We tend to have well-fashioned expectations about faith, how we think faith should be, certain in what we should believe.

This story reminds us that faith is not like that. To believe in Jesus sometimes requires a trip to Sychar, because there he might show you something that you need to see—about him and about yourself. It's not an easy journey. Jesus himself was tired and thirsty. And the sun can beat down on us mercilessly, exposing what we resist recognizing about ourselves, and sometimes even what we do not want to acknowledge about God. Going to Sychar is an essential part of faith if we are to realize fully what it means that God so loved the world, and especially if you have forgotten how much God loves you. "It is necessary to go through Samaria" to find ourselves once again and to be found once again by the one who loves us so much.

Prayer

Dear Jesus, you take us on hard journeys some days, to places we do not want to go, to see things we do not want to see, to people whom we do not want to meet. When you say "follow me," give us the courage and strength to do so. Amen.

Notes to Self

Chapter Two

Wonder

*She is beautiful. But you really cannot comprehend it until you understand
that she is the result of the pieces that she refused to let life take from her.*

—JmStorm

Focus Verses: John 4:7-15

⁷A Samaritan woman came to the well to draw water. Jesus said to
her, "Give me some water to drink." ⁸His disciples had gone into the city
to buy him some food. ⁹The Samaritan woman asked, "Why do you, a Jewish man, ask for something to drink from me, a Samaritan woman?" (Jews
and Samaritans didn't associate with each other.) ¹⁰Jesus responded, "If
you recognized God's gift and who is saying to you, 'Give me some water
to drink,' you would be asking him and he would give you living water."
¹¹The woman said to him, "Sir, you don't have a bucket and the well is
deep. Where would you get this living water? ¹²You aren't greater than our
father Jacob, are you? He gave this well to us, and he drank from it himself, as did his sons and his livestock." ¹³Jesus answered, "Everyone who
drinks this water will be thirsty again, ¹⁴but whoever drinks from the water
that I will give will never be thirsty again. The water that I give will become in those who drink it a spring of water that bubbles up into eternal

life." [15]The woman said to him, "Sir, give me this water, so that I will never be thirsty and will never need to come here to draw water!"

Read

Read the following passages in the Gospel of John. Note how they illustrate the five themes discussed in the *Introduction* (rebirth/new creation; identity of Jesus; relationship; witness; abundance) and the connections you are making to the *Focus Verses*.

John 2:1-11

John 6:1-71

John 7:37-39

John 10:1-10

John 19:31-37

John 21:1-19

Review

Finally, the conversation begins! In this section of the conversation, we overhear the initial encounter between Jesus and the Samaritan woman at the well. Once again, there are several details worth our attention. Not only do these details provide important information when it comes to understanding the many levels of the conversation going forward, but they also beg our response. They invite us into the story. We are not bystanders watching idly by but find ourselves as partners in the dialogue. We are asked to imagine how we might react to Jesus's statements. How would we respond to Jesus's questions? What might our answers be, and our questions be, were we to picture ourselves sitting on the well wall with Jesus?

"A Samaritan woman came to the well to draw water" (John 4:7)

There she is, minding her own business, fetching water from the well, as she is required to do, typically twice a day. Yet there is something wrong with this picture. No one goes to the well to draw water in the heat of the day. Women expected to provide water for their immediate family went to the well in the early morning when the sun has barely had time to rise and at dusk when the sun has fallen just below the horizon. Because of the Palestinian climate, dawn and dusk were the opportune times for this chore. As Jesus has just been in Jerusalem to celebrate Passover, and is now traveling back to Galilee through Samaria, the conversation is likely taking place sometime between late March and the end of April. It should be surprising that the woman comes to the well at noon. Why is she there at that time?

You have likely read somewhere or heard from some preacher that the reason she had to go to the well at noon was that she was a sinner, an outcast, having had five husbands and now cohabitating with a man who is not her husband. No one, therefore, wants to associate with this sinful, immoral woman, who either has bad taste in men or is "loose," as some are wont to say. We will see in chapter three that there is no basis for thinking of the Samaritan woman in this way. The story never comments on her sinfulness—in fact, sin never appears in the passage at all! Jesus never condemns her or judges her. And while a number of interpretations of this passage insist that Jesus forgives her of her many sins, there is nothing about forgiveness anywhere in the story. To make these assumptions about her is to read conclusions into the passage that are simply not there. These suppositions also betray contemporary biases against women, particularly around sexuality, that would not have existed in the first century. We will talk about this much more in the next chapter, but for the time being, let's suspend such biases and pay attention to what actually gets said in the story.

In chapter 1, we noted the comparison between Nicodemus and the Samaritan woman at the well, that Nicodemus meets Jesus at night and the woman at the well meets Jesus at noon. Rather than predispose her to sin, we take a clue from John's Gospel itself which has already set up the important metaphor of light and darkness. Since Jesus is the light of the world, the light shining in the darkness, and light represents being open to and in a relationship with Jesus, we might wonder at this point what she will see in Jesus—and what Jesus might see in her—when the sun is at its highest in the sky. What will be revealed between the two of them, when neither can hide in the shadows, when both are exposed? What possibilities might there be for her, meeting the Light of the World at the brightest time of the day? The story begs inquiry, not forgone conclusion or condemnation. The time of the day indicates possibility and purpose, not prejudice and prejudgment.

John tells us that a "Samaritan" woman came to draw water. We are in Samaria, so the fact that she is a Samaritan woman seems obvious. Why tell us this about her? For John, it's a way of emphasizing the surprise of the situation, even the shock of such an encounter. Think of the "good Samaritan" story (Luke 10:25-37). The shock of that parable is that it's the Samaritan, not the priest or the Levite, who helps the dying guy in the ditch. Just in case we forgot, we are indeed in Samaria, where no Jew should be, especially Jesus, who is a Jewish man with religious authority, as Nicodemus assumed. This encounter will be a surprise indeed, on many levels, and, for all intents and purposes, should not be happening.

Jesus is the first to speak at this well-side encounter, requesting a drink. Jesus begins the unconventional conversation, setting aside society norms. Social convention is not how the kingdom of God works. Remember John 3:16? He has already crossed into Samaria. Boundary crossing is just beginning. Jesus's need for a drink also foreshadows his words from the cross, "I am thirsty" (John 19:28), reminding us that, yes, Jesus is human. While Jesus will reveal his true identity as God to the woman at the well later in their exchange, here the truth of his identity is God—*in the flesh*.

"His disciples had gone into the city to buy him some food" (4:8)

In many Bibles, this phrase is in parentheses. While, grammatically speaking, parentheses enclose a word, clause, or sentence inserted as an explanation or afterthought into a passage that is grammatically complete without it, a parenthetical remark is never something to overlook when it comes to reading the Bible. We are prone to pass over parentheses often when reading, usually for the sake of time. After all, a parenthetical remark is a postscript, an addendum, information we don't need to make sense of what we are reading. However, no parentheses or any other punctuation were included in the original manuscripts of the biblical writings. In fact, the original copies we have of the Bible—that is, as close as we can get to the original because the oldest manuscript we have of the New Testament, for example, dates back to the fourth century—do not have chapters, verses, paragraphing, titles, punctuation, or even spaces between words! All of these features were added later in manuscript copying to procure a readable text.

The fact that the disciples leave Jesus at the well and head off to the city to buy some food again emphasizes the scandal of this encounter. Jesus and the Samaritan woman at the well should not be meeting like this, or in any circumstances, for that matter. In doing so, they are crossing just about every boundary put in place for the sake of good social order—societal, political, cultural, and religious. A man would never be alone with a woman other than his wife—and vice versa. A Jew would never be alone with a Samaritan. A rabbi, a Jewish religious leader such as Jesus, would never be alone with a woman. The woman's response to Jesus's request for a drink underscores this forbidden encounter, "Why do you, a Jewish man, ask for something to drink from me, a Samaritan woman?" (John 4:9). Likely from his appearance, she knows him to be a Jew. But there's way more going on here. The punctuation in the NRSVue captures the scandal of the situation, "How is it that you, a *Jew*, ask a drink of *me*, a *woman* of *Samaria*?" (italics added for emphasis). Can't you just hear her? She calls out the issue, naming the restrictions set in place to prevent such prohibited behavior. Perhaps she is inquisitive, perhaps she is rightly concerned about the possible ramifications of this meeting, or perhaps she is truly stunned. How might you inflect her question? Her response gives voice to the trappings of her society—the boundaries and borders that separated peoples at that time, that oppressed her in particular—and still do today.

The incredulity of this meeting calls to mind the calling of the disciples, where the central verb is that of "finding" (reread John 1:35-51). While the verb "to find" is not used in John 4, Jesus "had to go through Samaria" to find a disciple, to find a witness, to fulfill John 3:16, but it also looks forward to Jesus's finding of the man born blind in John 10:16. Jesus, the Good Shepherd that he is, finds the man when he was cast out, bringing him into the Good Shepherd's fold (John 9:35). How is this also true for the woman at the well? She is at the well at noon, cast out from her counted-on societal structures and relationships, alone, and yet Jesus finds her. Of all the people in the world Jesus could seek after, he places his hope in a despised people and in this rejected, nameless woman.

"Jews and Samaritans didn't associate with each other"—or in the NRSVue, "Jews do not share things in common with Samaritans"—is also often found in parentheses in our modern-day Bibles. Like "his disciples had gone into the city to him some buy food," don't skip over this parenthetical comment. It is a detail that highlights how astonishing this conversation truly is. It is also just about the biggest understatement of the Bible. To come in contact with a Samaritan, in Judaism at that time, would render you unclean. This is not about hospitality or an indictment of not apportioning your abundance or that the Jews and the Samaritans needed to learn how to share. Quite simply and literally, Jews and Samaritans did not have any contact, whatsoever, at all, especially physical contact, period. And here's Jesus, asking for a cup of water. And you have to wonder if he even brought his own glass.

In fact, Jesus does intend to share with her, offering her his gift of living water, his very own self (John 7:37-39). But this overture of Jesus's very own self is what gets misunderstood, just as it happened with Nicodemus. When Jesus says to Nicodemus, "I assure you, unless someone is born anew, it's not possible to see God's kingdom" (John 3:3), Jesus presents Nicodemus with the chance to be reborn, to be a child of God, as promised back in John 1:12-13. Nicodemus's literal response is almost comical, "How is it possible for an adult to be born? It's impossible to enter the mother's womb for a second time and be born, isn't it?" (John 3:4). The Greek word that gets translated "born anew" ("from above" in the NRSVue) is deliberately ambiguous because it can be rendered "from above," "again," and "anew." Nicodemus equates "being born" with actual birth, unable to recognize the relationship Jesus is offering. The reaction of the woman at the well is similar to that of Nicodemus in that she answers Jesus's statement on a kind of literal level. She states the obvious, "Excuse me, sir, but I don't see you having a bucket, and have you looked down in that well? It's a deep one!" These moments of misunderstanding between Jesus and his conversation partners are common occurrences in the Gospel of John. Characters frequently misconstrue what Jesus is saying or what Jesus is offering. Some commentators suggest that Jesus is trying to trick or test people, which does not make for a very appealing Jesus. This is not Jesus being antagonistic, but invitational. The encounters Jesus has with individuals are meant to lead to an intimate relationship with him and with God. The initial miscomprehension indicates that this abiding relationship with Jesus and with God is not something that we are actually capable of understanding, and especially not right away. Comprehension is not the hoped-for goal, but rather entering into a conversation that might lead to relationship, even though we do not fully understand what it all means. Part of being a disciple is to step into the relationship, continually, no matter what and not waiting for graspable explanations. The question here, therefore, is whether the woman at the well will stay in the conversation longer than Nicodemus. And the question for us is, will we? Conversation is a critical component of any relationship. It is in conversation that we learn, that we get to know someone. Shouldn't that also be true when it comes to our relationship with God?

"You aren't greater than our father Jacob, are you?" (4:12)

With this question, the woman at the well already moves beyond Jesus's conversation with Nicodemus. Whereas Nicodemus got stuck in the literal, asking, "how can these things be?" the woman at the well has another question for Jesus, "And just who do you think you are?" Unbeknownst to her, her question addresses one of the most important themes we noted for the Gospel of John: Jesus's identity. The theme of Jesus's identity gets introduced back at the very beginning of the Gospel, in the very first verse of the Gospel, "In the beginning was the Word, / and the Word was with God, and the Word was God" (John 1:1). Jesus is the Word made flesh (John 1:14), this unique, one-and-only, begotten God (John 1:18). It is Jesus's identity that will be revealed to her—in time and if she remains in the conversation long enough.

The inquiry of the woman at the well, "You aren't greater than our father Jacob, are you?" in fact speaks truth; Jesus is greater than Jacob. She is attempting to make sense of who Jesus could be, and in light of their shared ancestry. While there is a rift between the Jews and the Samaritans at the time of Jesus, they both trace their roots back to Abraham and his descendants. This well was the source of water—even the source of life—for Jacob, his family, and his livestock. Who could Jesus be, if their forefather relied on this well for water? Once again, Jesus's answer is not a test or a trap but intends to draw her further into dialogue: "Everyone who drinks this water will be thirsty again, but whoever drinks from the water that I will give will never be thirsty again. The water that I give will become in those who drink it a spring of water that bubbles up into eternal life" (John 4:13-14). Who wouldn't be curious after a statement like that? Jesus wants her to realize that water itself, why she came to the well in the first place, is not the issue. Like the signs—turning water into wine and feeding five thousand people—it's what the signs point to that really matters. Jesus wants her to see who he really is and what he has to offer. Jesus is the source of abundant water—she will never be thirsty—and dependence on his water leads to a relationship with him and with God that will never be broken.

"a spring of water that bubbles up into eternal life" (4:14)

The Samaritan woman at the well has already advanced farther in her conversation with Jesus than Nicodemus. Jesus's response acknowledges her curiosity, maybe even her tenacity, her openness, her wondering. Jesus tells her the truth about the well, and any well. Wells eventually dry up. After a while, you're going to have to dig another one. The water Jesus offers, however, is like an underground spring—think Old Faithful Geyser in Yellowstone National Park. A spring that never runs dry. In Greek, "bubbles up" indicates an ongoing reality, a perpetual state. The Greek verb communicates an unending source of water. Jesus is not saying he is better than Jacob. Such readings move dangerously close to anti-Semitism. Jesus is not sent to replace Judaism, nor does the Jesus movement—a community of believers within Judaism—supersede Judaism or question God's commitment to God's people, the Israelites. Jesus as the Word made flesh is the embodiment of John 3:16, "God so loved the world," and that means the whole world. Jesus wants the Samaritan woman to know here what he will promise later: "On the last and most important day of the festival, Jesus stood up and shouted, 'All who are thirsty should come to me! / All who believe in me should drink! / As the scriptures said concerning me, / rivers of living water will flow out from within him'" (John 7:37-38). The festival to which John is referring is the Festival of Booths or Tabernacles. One of the ceremonies during the Feast of Booths is the water ceremony, reminding the people of God's provision of water in the wilderness (Exodus 17:1-7). Jesus travels to Jerusalem for this pilgrimage feast (John 7:2, 14), and during the celebration of Sukkoth, Jesus identifies himself as the same living water that sustained God's people in the wilderness. At Jesus's death, his very body will be a source of water, "one of the soldiers pierced his side with a spear, and immediately blood and water came out" (John 19:34).

Jesus provides us with what we need for our daily lives to be sustained. Like a good parent, Jesus makes sure his children (John 1:12-13) have everything they need. As we read further along in John's Gospel, Jesus will identify himself as the "bread of life" (see John 6). When Jesus feeds the five thousand people, it is not just a miracle, but a sign to show us that Jesus is the bread of life from heaven. Jesus provides us with ever-flowing water (Exodus 17:1-7) and daily bread, just like the manna from the sky for God's people in the wilderness (Exodus 16:1-36; Numbers 11:1-9). In John 10, Jesus describes himself as the Good Shepherd, who leads his sheep out to pasture, because with Jesus, there is abundant life: "I came so that they could have life—indeed, so that they could live life to the fullest" (John 10:10). Abundant life is exactly what Jesus is offering the woman at the well. This abundance comes from the true intention of God, to which the Fourth Evangelist testifies, "From his fullness we have all received grace upon grace" (John 1:16). Not just a little "grace" or "some grace," but grace upon grace. This abundance becomes most evident in the signs of Jesus. Each of the signs is over the top. At the wedding at Cana (John 2:1-11), six jars, each holding twenty-thirty gallons of water, were filled to the brim with the best wine when nobody expected it. Weddings in first-century Palestine lasted about a week. As the story indicates, the good wine was served first (think of your favorite thirty-dollar bottle of Chardonnay), when the guests were sober, and the mediocre wine at best (think Gallo or Inglenook jug) later, when the guests want to keep drinking but don't really care what they drink. Jesus's very first act in his public ministry is a sign of abundant proportions.

In John 5, Jesus heals a man who has not been able to walk for thirty-eight years, which, in first-century Palestine, would have been that man's entire lifetime. The blind man who has his sight restored in John 9 has been blind since birth. Signs of abundant proportions. The raising of Lazarus (John 11) would be miraculous enough and yet Lazarus has been dead four days. Jewish belief asserted that the soul left the body after three days. Lazarus being dead four days means that he is really, really dead, no question about it, and yet Jesus calls to Lazarus and he walks out of the tomb. Finally, at the last resurrection appearance in John 21, it is not until the disciples catch an abundance of fish after Jesus's direction to cast their nets on the other side of the boat that they recognize Jesus standing on the shore (John 21:6-7). Recognition of Jesus's identity happens in and through abundance. Jesus is the giver of abundant life—new life, new creation, new birth. And abundant life is also eternal life. They are one in the same—relationship with Jesus. If you ever needed a definition for eternal life, look no further than John's Gospel: "This is eternal life: to know you, the only true God, and Jesus Christ whom you sent" (John 17:3).

Jesus is offering the Samaritan woman what she needs—water— essential for life and survival. And yet, Jesus is offering her so much more—life abundant ("What came into being through the Word was life," John 1:3-4), his very self. This she has yet to see, she has yet to recognize, but she's getting there. In fact, at this point in the conversation she has advanced in her recognition of who Jesus is. At first, Jesus is a thirsty Jew with bad manners—after all, he doesn't even say "please" when he asks her for a drink! But at this point in the conversation, something has changed for her. Clearly, there is not full perception of Jesus's identity—there is so much more to see! But she has made a small step ahead, acknowledging, without full understanding, that Jesus has something that she needs. This progression is not unlike the gradual perception of the formerly blind man of Jesus in John 9. The man's spiritual sight moves from seeing Jesus as "the man they call Jesus" (John 9:11), to "he's a prophet" (John 9:17), to "from God" (John 9:33), and then, "Lord, I believe" (John 9:38), and he worships Jesus. We will witness a similar progression of "sight" by the woman at the well, but she is not quite there yet. The conversation must continue—there's still more to be said, more to be discovered. And so, her request of Jesus, "Sir, give me this water," is still on a literal level. To paraphrase, "Wait a minute. You mean I wouldn't have to schlep my bucket to the well twice a day? I'll take it!" But she is open. There is an expression and recognition of need. On the one hand, she is still engaging with Jesus on a literal level, but on the other hand, she is now farther along than Nicodemus. She wonders. She has not shut the door on possibility, and so the conversation will continue. Jesus sees to that.

Reflect, Respond, Renew

Reflect

The Samaritan woman at the well names the cultural boundaries of her day that maintained the norms of her society. We have many of those kinds of edifices in our own lives. We might get to Sychar, either intentionally or accidentally, but once we are there, we've often already sized up the people we meet based on race, gender, ethnicity, religion, demography, education, sexual orientation, age, and ability—all before any conversation is shared. This is part of how our society works, so it's hard to admit and it's hard to escape. This portion of John 4 reminds us of how much we go about our lives with assumptions about people, thereby shutting down conversation rather than entering into dialogue. A quote attributed to Carl Jung goes like this, "Thinking is difficult, that's why most people judge."

Respond

What do you see as some of those borders in your life? Where and when are those boundaries built for safety, and where and when are those boundaries put in place to separate? Can you think of a time when you met someone and immediately judged before going any further in a potential conversation? Our first impressions size up the situation, shutting down possibility. We all know the phrase, "you can't judge a book by its cover." How might this story change a situation like that for you going forward?

Reflect

The response of the woman at the well to Jesus, "Why do you, a Jewish man, ask for something to drink from me, a Samaritan woman?" (John 4:9), reveals that she knows her place very well and no one has ever let her forget it. She is a woman, not worthy of address, and she is a Samaritan, an outsider, unclean, reviled. Society has determined her value and there have likely been few circumstances in her life where she's been able to imagine anything different. "How can you be talking to me? How can I possibly be worth your time?" Maybe those are the questions that swirled around in her mind when she questioned Jesus's proprieties. "How is it that you could possibly need anything from me, Jesus?" And yet, Jesus found her; Jesus chose her, "You didn't choose me, but I chose you and appointed you so that you could go and produce fruit and so that your fruit could last" (John 15:16).

Respond

Might these also be your questions? Have you questioned your own worth, your own significance and purpose in the world? Our society places so many expectations on us; these ideals are not achievable, and yet we still strive for them anyway. How we look, how much we weigh, how much money we make. Expectations of beauty, productivity, and education. Our careers and achievements. What are some of those expectations you are trying to live up to? Where do they come from? Jesus doesn't care about any of that. If he did, he would have never gone to Samaria in the first place. At that well, Jesus wants the woman to come to a recognition of who he is. But Jesus also wants her to come to a recognition of who she is—enough.

Reflect

The Samaritan woman has to go alone, is forced to go alone, to the well. After all, who wants to be around her? "Five husbands? Girlfriend, that is some bad luck you've had. I don't want it to rub off on me." Snubbed and shunned, she makes her way along that dirt path, yoked with empty buckets that might seem light now, but will soon be heavy with the weight of water and the shame and blame that have cast her aside. We can try and hide out in Sychar or come to the well alone when we hope nobody is looking. But nothing is going to prevent God from loving the world, from loving you, even with all the times we've made John 3:16 a threat rather than a promise. Nothing is going to prevent God from finding the witness

God needs. Remember, Jesus finds her—he has to go through Samaria, or as the King James Version says, "he must needs go through Samaria" (John 4:4). And there, he asks for what he needs, a drink. Not Jesus at his Miss Manners best, mind you. But you never know when a sip of water might lead to a long conversation where Jesus tells you your truth. "I see that your well has run dry."

Respond

Are there times when you have felt alone, shamed, and blamed, which makes it almost impossible to hear what Jesus is offering you? In those moments, we often default to second guesses about ourselves, just like the woman at the well. She knows her place, and no one has ever let her forget it. Have you been taught to know and keep your place, not able to believe that God could use you to further God's kingdom? By whom? The church? Family members? A partner? This story assures us of Jesus's belief in us and his trust in us. "How is it that you, Jesus, could need something from me?" we say. But Jesus responds, "You didn't choose me, but I chose you" (John 15:16). Jesus found you, remember? Consider this quote, author unknown: "No matter what you do, someone will always talk about you. Someone will always question your judgement. Someone will always doubt you. So just smile and make the choices you can live with."

Reflect

Oftentimes we make excuses for ourselves as not worthy of God's attention. We would not be alone in this activity. Many biblical characters, when approached by God, have the same reaction. God finds Abraham and Sarah. Abraham says he's too old. Sarah laughs. God finds Moses, and what does Moses say? "I haven't taken Intro to Public Speaking yet." God finds Jeremiah, and what does Jeremiah say? "Sorry, God. I am way too young." This is what we do. Make excuses. Offer God lame arguments as to why God got it all wrong. "I'm sorry, God. You could not possibly need me." When I went to seminary, the joke was, "Here I am, Lord. Send somebody else." As if God made a mistake. Other times, we just misunderstand. And we are in good company in that, too. Remember, when Jesus says to Nicodemus, "you have to be born again," Nicodemus's response? "What? You want me to go into my mother's womb and be born again? That's gonna hurt." And when Jesus offers the woman at the well living water, her response? "Uh, sir. I'm not seeing that you have a bucket—and have you looked down in that well? You should. 'Cause it's deep."

The well is often deep, all right. That water that quenches our thirst, that gives voice again to dry mouths, that makes for parched lips to speak again, often seems so very out of reach. We peer down in that well, that cavernous, yawning, bottomless hole, wondering how long it will take for the bucket to reach the bottom and if it is even worth it to try. Yes, we are thirsty, desperately so. But sometimes the efforts to satisfy the longings of our souls seem too terribly far away, impossible even, to reach.

Respond

What do you do for yourself when you feel like the well is too deep, that the nourishment you need, the support you need, the encouragement you need, is just too far away? What excuses do you make—not to take care of yourself, not to follow your dreams, not to live into the life to which God is calling you? Maybe now is the time to "gather up all your scattered dreams and build the life you love" (author unknown). What would it take to put those excuses aside and follow what you feel called to do? What would it take to come out of the tombs that confine you? When and why can't you hear your name being called, "Lazarus, come out!" (John 11:43); "Mary!" (John 20:16)?

Reflect

This story reminds us, and Jesus reminds us, that wells also dry up. Eventually, you have to dig a new well, hoping to tap a water source once again. There is no feeling quite like that of being tapped out. But then Jesus says, "The water I will give you will never run out, never dry up. It will gush up, eternally, like a fountain, like a geyser, like an underground spring." "Awesome!" says the woman, "If I don't have to keep hauling this bucket here? Sign me up!" Her response may seem naïve, like more misunderstanding. Does she really get it? But Jesus is not something you get. Jesus is someone. Period. And someone takes a lot longer to understand, to know, than something. It's no accident that this encounter between Jesus and the woman at the well is a conversation. If Jesus just showed up and said, "Guess what? I'm God!" I don't imagine the story would have been the same.

Respond

When have you felt that feeling? That feeling of being completely tapped out? What were the circumstances? What led to that situation? Is it something that you think could have been prevented? Or do you know what you might do differently if that situation arises again? One thing that the woman at the well does is open herself up to possibility. She recognizes that maybe, just maybe, Jesus has something she needs—yes, that water for which she is responsible, day after day. But maybe, also, something that will get her *through* the day—the relationship for which she longs, which she has been denied far too long. The woman at the well asks. She questions. She wonders. Whom might you ask to help fill your well?

Renew

At this moment in the conversation, we wait and wonder, what will she say? Will the conversation continue or come to a screeching halt, as it did with Nicodemus? Her response could have been like that of Nicodemus, "how can these things be?" And so, the woman at the well gives us another key to unlocking our potential as disciples—wonder. There should be a signpost before going into this story that reads something like, "Questions and curiosity encouraged." Openness and wonder are hugely important for faith. It's hard, I know. So much of what has been told to us about faith insists on answers and certainty. Having the correct beliefs. Knowing certain confessions and creeds. To ask is risky. To admit you don't know something is to put yourself on the line. To admit that you can't do it alone is to admit that you don't want to be alone. But that's what relationship is all about. And that's what God most desperately wants—and with you.

Prayer

Dear Jesus, when the well is deep, and we are oh so tired. When the well is deep and there is not a drop left. When the well is deep, and the answers are not there, help us to lean into wonder. To voice questions we've been too afraid to ask. Remind us of this woman's curiosity and openness to possibility. Help us remember that a simple request is perhaps all that's necessary, "Jesus, Jesus? Give me that water," and who knows what might follow? Well, you do—life abundant. Amen.

Notes to Self

_____

_____

_____

_____

_____

_____

_____

_____

_____

_____

Trust

A bird sitting in a tree is never afraid of the branch breaking. Because her trust is not in the branch but in her wings.

—Unknown

Focus Verses: John 4:16-24

¹⁶Jesus said to her, "Go, get your husband, and come back here." ¹⁷The woman replied, "I don't have a husband." "You are right to say, 'I don't have a husband,'" Jesus answered. ¹⁸"You've had five husbands, and the man you are with now isn't your husband. You've spoken the truth."

¹⁹The woman said, "Sir, I see that you are a prophet. ²⁰Our ancestors worshipped on this mountain, but you and your people say that it is necessary to worship in Jerusalem." ²¹Jesus said to her, "Believe me, woman, the time is coming when you and your people will worship the Father neither on this mountain nor in Jerusalem. ²²You and your people worship what you don't know; we worship what we know because salvation is from the Jews. ²³But the time is coming—and is here!—when true worshippers will worship in spirit and truth. The Father looks for those who worship him this way. ²⁴God is spirit, and it is necessary to worship God in spirit and truth."

Read

Read the following passages in the Gospel of John. Note how they illustrate the five themes discussed in the *Introduction* (rebirth/new creation; identity of Jesus; relationship; witness; abundance) and the connections you are making to the *Focus Verses*.

John 2:13-21

John 9:1-41

John 20:19-31

Review

Already the woman at the well has moved farther along in her conversation with Jesus than Nicodemus. Because of her openness to Jesus's offerings, even though she does not quite understand what it all means, nor should she, Jesus takes the conversation to the next level. Jesus sees in her that she can take the next step in realizing who Jesus is and what he has to offer her. In her wonder, he sees her potential. This next part of the conversation is not manipulation on the part of Jesus. He is not trying to trick her or expose her. Rather, Jesus wants her, even needs her, to grow in her awareness of who is standing before her—the Word made flesh, the very presence of God. Jesus knows the truth about her life, but he is not getting her to admit that truth to shame her or blame her. Jesus's request is not about forcing her to confess her sins so that Jesus can forgive her, as we shall see. Rather, it is the moment for this relationship to grow deeper. The woman at the well has recognized that Jesus can provide what she went to the well to get—water. She has communicated openness to what else Jesus might have to offer. Jesus takes this wonder and runs with it.

This portion of the story of the Samaritan woman at the well is notoriously misinterpreted, typically by casting her in an unfair light. These readings focus on her sinfulness and her questionable morality, assuming it's her fault that she's had five husbands. I have no doubt that you have heard or read some disparaging titles given to her: "five-time loser," "tramp," "promiscuous," and "adulterous." Twenty-first-century biases about women get piled onto this particular woman. It is important to name what's going on here—sexism, which is prejudice, stereotyping, or discrimination against women; and misogyny, which is dislike, even hatred, of women. Particularly, these readings view women as the reason that men go astray or that marriages fall apart. She's had five husbands because "she can't make her man happy," her sexual prowess cannot be resisted, or she is a seductress. We see the blaming and shaming of women in commentaries on the story of Adam and Eve too. In these interpretations, Eve seduced Adam into eating the apple and it was Eve's fault they got kicked out of the garden. Of course, Adam had every chance to speak up, but he didn't say a word. There are strands in biblical interpretation that are deeply sexist and misogynist. These perspectives use the Bible to argue against women having any kind of leadership roles in churches, even that women should not read in church. An often-cited passage comes from Paul's first letter to the Corinthians: "Like in all the churches of God's people, the women should be quiet during the meeting. They are not allowed to talk. Instead, they need to get under control, just as the Law says. If they want to learn something, they should ask their husbands at home. It is disgraceful for a woman to talk during the meeting" (1 Corinthians 14:33b-35). This passage is held up to justify the subordination of women. Another passage is, "A wife should learn quietly with complete submission. I don't allow a wife to teach or to control her husband. Instead, she should be a quiet listener. Adam was formed first, and then Eve. Adam wasn't deceived, but rather his wife became the one who stepped over the line because she was completely deceived" (1 Timothy 2:11-14), when in other letters, Paul names women as ministry partners in the spread of the Gospel (like Phoebe, Prisca, and Junia in Romans 16; Chloe in 1 Corinthians 1:11; Euodia and Syntyche in Philippians 4:2). Interpretations of Scripture that seek to blame or silence women contend that women are the second sex, subpar, and should be subservient to men, especially their husbands. Validation for such claims is also based on the creation story—Eve was created second—and on the household codes and the structure of a typical Roman household in the first century, adopted in New Testament writings (Colossians 3:12–4:6; Ephesians 5:21–6:9; 1 Timothy 6:1-2; 1 Peter 2:11–3:22). These codes, however, were not meant for all future household structures, but rather represent the patriarchal culture of Greco-Roman society. The male was the head of the household with women, children, and slaves—yes, slaves—subordinate. Why is it that some passages are held up as proof for the roles of women in society and others, like those of the woman at the well, are ignored? When consulting commentaries on this passage, we want to sift out those that seek to uphold patriarchy and misogyny. Interpretations of the Bible that view groups of persons "less than" in God's eyes do not have the heart of divine love.

"Go, get your husband, and come back here" (John 4:16)

Tone is everything when it comes to these opening verses of this section of the dialogue. How do you imagine Jesus speaking these words? Do you hear Jesus being accusatory? If so, is that really how you imagine Jesus to be? Or might we imagine Jesus uttering these words in a caring, empathetic tone of voice? Either way tells us a lot about who we think Jesus is—and how we think Jesus might interact with us. Do you really believe that Jesus would speak to you this way? Sometimes, we are apt to forget that how we perceive Jesus's behavior in a particular story of the New Testament is also how Jesus could respond to and act with us. And we can't forget that the reason Jesus went to Sychar in the first place was because of love (John 3:16).

If Jesus's request of the woman at the well, "go, get your husband, and come back here," comes from Jesus's heart—an understanding heart and not trying to humiliate, a heart full of love and not pity, a heart filled with empathy and not seeking to embarrass—no wonder the woman answers truthfully. She is not evasive or defensive. She doesn't beat around the bush, hemming and hawing, trying to come up with a clever answer or one that might deflect the issue. Maybe she sensed in Jesus's bidding his concern and compassion. As a result, she speaks her truth. She is honest: "I don't have a husband." In Jesus's response to her truth, considering the tone is again essential—is it harsh and biting? Or gentle and knowing? We might imagine Jesus's answer to sound something like this, "I know. I know. I know your plight. I know the indignity and dishonor with which you have had to live so much of your life. I know the sorrow you have had to endure. And I am so very sorry." Jesus is not critical or judgmental or condemning. He knows her truth. He wants her to recognize him as the Truth—and the truth of who she could be.

Awareness of the historical situation of the woman at the well is critical for faithful interpretation of her story. The fact that she had five husbands is a situation completely out of her control. A woman in first-century Palestine had little to no agency when it came to her marital life. While a man could divorce his wife for the smallest of reasons, a woman could not instigate divorce. One of the explanations for Jesus's concern about divorce is that men were divorcing their wives over virtually nothing, thus leaving the woman potentially in a harmful and vulnerable state (see, for example, Mark 10:2-12). Women were dependent on a male provider, so either divorce or the death of the husband would put a woman in jeopardy. Given this information, the woman at the well had five husbands, not of her own doing, but because they either died, leaving her widowed (also, a very precarious situation, which is why there are directives for caring for widows in the Bible; see Deuteronomy 16:11-14; Psalm 68:5; Isaiah 10:1-3; Jeremiah 22:1-5; Ezekiel 22:6-7; Matthew 23:24; Luke 7:11-17; Acts 6; 1 Timothy 5; James 1:27), or divorced her. While a man could divorce his wife for causes of his own determination or on a whim, the primary purpose would be that she was barren, thus unable to provide him with an heir. This was, of course, the foremost motive for marriage in the ancient world—procreation and carrying on the family name. We should stop and imagine for a minute the cloud of disgrace, therefore, under which the woman at the well lived. She was incapable of fulfilling the one thing she was, at that time, put on the earth to do—have children. Many of us know that kind of shame today—the pain, even guilt, of infertility.

Her current living situation would have only exacerbated her guilt, pain, and shame. There was no such thing as "living together" before marriage or for convenience in the ancient world, even though commentators will still label her a "loose woman" for "shacking up" with some guy. The likely historical situation is that she was forced to live with her dead husband's brother, called a "levirate marriage," outlined by law in Deuteronomy 25:5-10. In this circumstance, the brother, or "levir," of the man (her husband) who died, if there were no children to care for the widow, was obligated to marry the widow. The marriage could be formal or informal. Often, the first child between them would be accounted to the deceased brother/husband to carry on his name. This law was set forth by God to protect women in these vulnerable circumstances. Otherwise, they would have nowhere to go. This is the full truth of this woman's life—five times either divorced or widowed, no children to take her in and support her, and now living with, and perhaps even married to, her dead husband's brother for the sake of her survival. This is the truth that Jesus knows and the truth that she shares—the truth that leads her to see Jesus as a prophet. The topic of the woman's husbands recalls the setting of conversation. Remember that the conversation takes place at Jacob's well, a betrothal scene in the Old Testament. I wonder in this moment if the woman at the well thought of her foremothers—Sarah, Rebekah, Leah, and Rachel. While Jesus and the woman at the well are not getting engaged here, we now realize that Jesus is offering her a relationship that she has never had, a partnership with him in which she will never again be abandoned or discarded.

"Sir, I see that you are a prophet" (4:19)

As a result of this loving exchange, the Samaritan woman moves yet another step forward in her realization of who Jesus could be—a prophet.

Recognizing Jesus to be a prophet will also be true for the man born blind: "Some of the Pharisees questioned the man who had been born blind again: 'What do you have to say about him, since he healed your eyes?' He replied, 'He's a prophet'" (John 9:17). The Pharisees had questioned the formerly blind man, wondering about Jesus: "Some Pharisees said, 'This man isn't from God, because he breaks the Sabbath law'" (John 9:16). The blind man perceives that indeed, that is the case—that Jesus is from God, a prophet sent by God—for how else could he have healed a man blind since birth? And on the Sabbath? Why, then, does the woman at the well believe that Jesus could be a prophet at this point in the dialogue? Because he knows her truth—her deepest, darkest, most painful truth, just like the prophets of old. The prophets of the Old Testament were God's messengers. They went to God's people, bringing a "word from the Lord." We assume, and incorrectly, that prophets were only forecasting the future. The prophets were only predictors of what was to come, however, insofar as they were able to assess the past and the present. We might imagine the prophets such as Isaiah and Jeremiah, Amos and Ezekiel, saying something like, "Okay, here's the deal, friends. If you keep going along like this, I am pretty sure that this is what's going to happen."

Part of the reason that Christians limit the role of biblical prophecy to prediction is because of how our Christian Old Testament is structured. The Old Testament in Christian Bibles begins with the Pentateuch, also called the *Torah* ("instruction"), or the Five Books of Moses; then, the General Writings, such as the Psalms (*Ketuvim*); then the prophetic books (*Nevi'im*). In Jewish Bibles, the prophetic books are second in canonical order. The General Writings are the last collection of books in the Jewish Scriptures because for Judaism, the prophetic books are considered historical books. That is, the prophets were sent from God to God's people at particular points in their history. The prophets spoke a word from the Lord to the Israelites that was truth-telling—about their situation, about their behavior, and where things could lead if they kept traveling the route they had chosen. But the prophets also voiced words of hope and encouragement. They weren't just naysayers, only preaching doom and gloom. When the relationship between God and the Israelites appeared to be going awry or was in question, like when the Israelites were in captivity under Babylonian rule, that's when God sent God's prophets—to bring God's people back to God toward reconciliation, mercy, and steadfast love. To assure God's people and give comfort—your God is here! God has not gone anywhere (Isaiah 40:10-11; 52:7-10). The Samaritan woman at the well sees in Jesus that very identity—the prophet who speaks truth, her truth. Maybe she even feels comforted and hears hope! And now she is but one step closer to knowing Jesus's truth—that he himself is the Truth (John 14:6). Their relationship has moved to the next level.

We need to underscore the point that Jesus knows her plight, not her sin. Nowhere does Jesus say she has sinned and nowhere in the story does Jesus forgive her of said sin. Remember from the Introduction that in the Gospel of John, sin is conceptualized in a very specific way. Like other theological topics or themes, sin is not uniformly defined in the Bible. How each writer conceives the meaning and function of sin is unique to that writer's perspective and purpose for writing. "Sin" in the Gospel of John does not have to do with one's morals or scruples. It's not about labeling what you have done wrong, but rather that you are apart from God, or not in a relationship with God/Jesus. When John the Baptist points to Jesus and says, "Look! The Lamb of God who takes away the sin of the world!" (John 1:29), note that "sin" is singular and not plural. Jesus comes into the world so that all might have a relationship with God. We might think of "sin" in the Gospel of John as not what you do (or don't do) but a state of being without God.

"neither on this mountain nor in Jerusalem" (4:21)

In this pastoral moment, the conversation moves to yet another level—when the woman at the well perceives Jesus to be a prophet. "Well then, Jesus, do I have a question for you!" Because when a prophet of God stands in front of you, you might have a few questions to ask!

Some interpretations of the woman's inquiry—"Our ancestors worshipped on this mountain, but you and your people say that it is necessary to worship in Jerusalem" (John 4:20)—suggest that she is trying to change the subject or move the focus away from "her sinful life." Yet, with the correct historical context in view, she is not deflecting the issue or being coy but asking a very important question, one that she thinks Jesus can answer. In fact, her question was the most pressing theological issue that separated the Jews and the Samaritans for centuries: the proper location for the worship of God. And for the author of the Gospel of John, this was also the theological crisis of post-70 CE Judaism. When the temple was destroyed by the Roman Empire in 70 CE, the center of Judaism was no more. God was believed to dwell in the innermost part of the temple, the place called the Holy of Holies. Only the High Priest on Yom Kippur, the Day of Atonement, was ever allowed behind the curtain into the Holy of Holies.

After the Babylonian captivity, the Jews built the Second Temple again in Jerusalem, but the Samaritans had already been constructing their temple in Samaria, on Mount Gerizim. If Jesus is a prophet, sent from God, then he would know which temple is valid for worshipping the Lord. In other words, she is asking something like, "Tell me, prophet, like the prophets of old who knew God, like Isaiah, Jeremiah, Hosea, Amos, Ezekiel, if you are a prophet, which temple is the place for true worship? Yours or mine?" In saying to Jesus, "Our ancestors worshipped on this mountain, but you and your people say that it is necessary to worship in Jerusalem" (John 4:20), she is not doing a little church shopping. She is not inquiring about a congregation that has the best programs, the best mission, the most members, the best band, or a coffee bar. "Jesus, what do you think? Should I go to Bethlehem Baptist? Nazareth Church of the Nativity? Christ Church in Capernaum?" No, the Samaritan woman puts forth the theological issue at the heart of where to worship—where is God? Since God resides in the temple, Jesus should have the inside scoop on which temple is legitimate. True worship of God is also a theological issue for Matthew, Mark, Luke, and John. In 70 CE, the temple and Jerusalem were razed, and one catastrophic result was the theological crisis: Where is God? For the authors of our four Gospels, the answer to that question is Jesus. Jesus is God's presence among us here and now—no longer in the temple. Each Gospel writer articulates this new presence of God and its meaning uniquely. For John, Jesus is the Word who was from the beginning, who became flesh and tented/tabernacled (John 1:14) among us as this unique, one-and-only, begotten God (John 1:18). Jesus is the "I AM" now in the world, not in any temple. Jesus answers the woman, therefore, with *his* truth—"Believe me, woman, the time is coming when you and your people will worship the Father neither on this mountain nor in Jerusalem" (John 4:21). True worship is not about a proper place or bona fide buildings. True worship means recognizing that in Jesus, God is standing before you. True worship is worshipping the Truth, "I am the way, the truth, and the life" (John 14:6), in spirit and truth.

Jesus wants the woman at the well to see that he is the temple now. So far in John's Gospel, we have already been given two clues that point to this revelation. The first clue came in the Prologue,

> The Word became flesh
> and made his home among us.
> We have seen his glory,
> glory like that of a father's only son,
> full of grace and truth. (John 1:14)

Your Bible might have the phrase "made his home among us" translated as "lived" or "dwelt." *The Message* renders it is as "moved into the neighborhood." Another possibility, and closest to the Greek word, is "tabernacled" or even "tented," recalling God's accompaniment of God's people in the wilderness. God was with God's people in those desert wanderings by means of the tabernacle, the portable temple containing the ark of the covenant, going wherever they went and never leaving them. John wants those who read this Gospel to realize that God is now tabernacling once again with us in Jesus. God is not in the temple but in the Word made flesh, Jesus.

A second clue indicating that God's presence is found in Jesus and not in the temple is the location of the temple incident/cleansing of the temple in the Gospel of John. In Matthew, Mark, and Luke, the temple bruhaha where Jesus enters the temple, overturns the tables, and yells, "stop making my Father's house a den of robbers/thieves" or a "hideout for crooks," occurs immediately after his entry into Jerusalem, or what we call Palm Sunday. For Matthew, Mark, and Luke, the skirmish in the temple is the tipping point to having Jesus arrested. In John, however, the temple incident gets moved to John 2:13-22, immediately after the wedding at Cana. It will be the raising of Lazarus from the dead that leads to Jesus's arrest in John (John 11:47-53). John has no problem relocating the temple event to the beginning of the story because its meaning lies not in its historicity but in what it reveals about who Jesus is. In John's case, we are to know up front that Jesus is the "I AM" among us. God will not be found in the temple, but in Jesus, God incarnated, the Word made flesh, the begotten God (John 1:18). When the Jewish leaders ask, "By what authority are you doing these things? What miraculous sign will you show us?" (John 2:18), Jesus answers them, "Destroy this temple and in three days I'll raise it up" (John 2:19). The Jewish leaders misunderstand Jesus, just like Nicodemus and the woman at the well, when they say, "It took forty-six years to build this temple, and you will raise it up in three days?" (John 2:20). The narrator then tells us plainly, "But the temple Jesus was talking about was his body" (John 2:21).

A central element of each encounter that Jesus has with someone in John's Gospel is whether that person will recognize Jesus as God, the only one whom you worship. And so, the man born blind "sees" much more than what physical sight can allow, "Jesus heard they had expelled the man born blind. Finding him, Jesus said, 'Do you believe in the Human One?' He answered, 'Who is he, sir? I want to believe in him.' Jesus said, 'You have seen him. In fact, he is the one speaking with you.' The man said,

'Lord, I believe.' And he worshipped Jesus" (John 9:35-38). During the trial narrative in John, it's incredibly sad when the Jewish authorities refuse the truth about Jesus, "We have no king except the emperor" (John 19:15). Other Bibles read, "we have no king but Caesar." In other words, they choose to worship the Roman emperor—and not God. They cannot see that in Jesus is their one true God. When Thomas meets the resurrected Jesus after declaring, "Unless I see the nail marks in his hands, put my finger in the wounds left by the nails, and put my hand into his side, I won't believe" (John 20:25), he sees and believes in Jesus's true identity when he testifies, "My Lord and my God!" (John 20:28).

At this juncture in the conversation, we are left wondering—will the woman at the well, like the man born blind, and like Thomas, see in Jesus his true identity? As her one and only God standing before her? It is a precipitous moment. She has come so far. In this portion of the conversation, we experience her ability to trust. She trusts Jesus with her truth. She trusts Jesus with her questions. She trusts Jesus to be the keeper of God's truth. Trust—the third key for unlocking your potential as a disciple of Jesus.

Reflect, Respond, Renew

Reflect

"Go call your husband." That's the kind of request that gets you in the very pit of your stomach, that feels like a punch in the gut. That feeling when you sense someone will learn your grimmest secrets. That feeling when you realize just how deeply buried is your self-blame. That feeling when you fear your shame will be revealed. What do you do in that moment? Feign ignorance? "I don't know what you're talking about, Jesus. Can you repeat that?" Pretend you didn't hear the question? "So, how was your Passover celebration this year? Mine was great!" Or do you simply tell the truth because there's nothing else to tell, nothing else to do. And the truth is less painful, in the end, than perpetuating lies. "I don't have a husband," the woman says.

It can be hard for us to tell the truth, to share our truth with others, especially with Jesus. But of course, Jesus knows it already. And with Jesus, there is no shaming or blaming, which our society likes to do. There is no judgment—which a lot of people love to do. Instead, Jesus has only compassion for her—and for us.

Respond

In her book *A Return to Love: Reflections on the Principles of "A Course in Miracles"* Marianne Williamson says, "It takes courage to endure the sharp pains of self-discovery, rather than choose to take the dull pain of unconsciousness that would last the rest of our lives." What truths about yourself are you hoping Jesus doesn't know, doesn't find out? What do you imagine Jesus would do and say about it if you met face to face? What difference might it make to remember that Jesus is aware of the truths we hide and loves us regardless? How might you live differently? Would you talk to Jesus more if you remembered that Jesus has only concern and love for you, like the woman at the well?

Reflect

The amount of interpretive ink still being spilled to browbeat the woman at the well already burdened by her times and her circumstances could likely fill your local library. We must call out the sexism that determines so much of how the Bible is read. The Bible is still used to silence and subordinate women. Some churches say that women cannot be preachers or pastors. In many households, the husband is considered the head of the family, with the wife having to be submissive to her husband, doing whatever he asks, following all his rules, meeting all his expectations. In too many of these cases, the Bible is misused to justify domestic abuse. Women stay in these abusive relationships because they are told they need to be "obedient to God's Word." These applications of

Scripture are incorrect because they take passages out of context—just as interpretations of the woman at the well have been taken out of her context. They are hurtful and harmful, even deadly. Is that God's intention for the use of God's Word?

As discussed above, a woman in first-century Palestine had no control over her marital status. Why did she have five husbands? Well, either they died or divorced her. She doesn't have the right to file for divorce. She doesn't get to wait to marry until she falls in love. She marries for survival. And if her husbands die or divorce her? She is bound by laws meant to care for the widow and at the mercy of any man who would marry her. Women today face very different circumstances and generally have many more options for self-determination. Those of us living in the twenty-first century too often fail to situate the Samaritan woman in her actual context and instead wrongly imagine possibilities for her that simply did not exist.

Respond

Have you ever experienced a time when the Bible was used against you—to judge or condemn your behavior, or even to judge who you are? How about a time when you have heard the Bible used to condemn others? Did you say anything? Why was it important for that person, church, or group to say that about you or about someone else, and what does it communicate about who they think God is? Does this discussion help you imagine how you might respond to a similar situation in the future? As someone once said, you don't have to show up at every argument to which you are invited. I like this, which comes from a presentation by Brené Brown: "When someone spews something really hurtful don't pick it up and hold it and rub it into your heart and snuggle with it and carry it around for a long time. Don't even put energy into kicking it to the curb. You gotta see it and step OVER it or go AROUND it and keep on going." You can keep going because the story of the woman at the well reminds us of the compassionate, loving, merciful God we worship.

Reflect

We know that one of the reasons for the woman at the well having had five husbands could have been divorce. She might have been divorced because she was unable to fulfill the only role that gave her worth in her societal context—bearing children. Continuing to add generations and carrying on the family name were primary societal values at that time. If a marriage was childless, the woman was assumed to be responsible and was seen as "worth" less. While the pressure for progeny is still present in our day, it does not have the same gravity as it did for a woman in the first century. At the same time, bearing children remains a societal expectation. Women today feel guilt and shame if they are unable to conceive a child, and women who choose not to have children are judged.

Respond

Have either you or someone you know experienced infertility or the demands to have children? How might this story and Jesus's interaction with the woman at the well speak into your own grief or that of someone you know? There is also still shame and guilt around divorce in our society, regardless of who filed, if it was amicable or not, and if there are children or not. Even the friendliest divorce leaves behind pain and loss. Divorce touches all of our lives in one manner or another. In trusting relationships, "Sometimes you just need to talk about something, not to get sympathy or help, but just to kill its power by allowing the truth of things to hit the air" (Karen Salmansohn). Often when we have guilt or shame, we bury the cause. We don't talk about it. And our silence is reinforced by our culture, where so many topics, like infertility and divorce, seem to be off limits for polite conversation. How does the honest and trusting interaction between Jesus and the Samaritan woman illustrate a different approach? Does it help or give you hope?

Reflect

It's no accident that this conversation takes place at Jacob's well, a betrothal scene in the Old Testament. The backdrop adds to the tenderness of the story, highlighting the fact that she is without a husband and likely without children. And yet, she draws water at the well of her ancestors, the promised lineage to Abraham. Jesus finds her to offer her a relationship she's never had and a life she's never been able to live. It's as if Jesus says to her, "I will not leave you. I will not abandon you. I will not forsake you. I came that you may have life and have it abundantly. You can trust me." Jesus wants her to have what she wants and what she needs—relationship. The solid foundation of any relationship is trust. Trust is hard because it is risky. When trust is not earned, hurt may result. When trust is broken, it's hard to imagine its repair. And trust has to be mutual.

Respond

Relationship is at the heart of who we are as humans and, according to John, at the heart of discipleship. This is what Jesus offers in John—not a how-to manual for faith, not a list of commandments for how to get into heaven, but an intimate and lasting relationship with him that finds its truest expression in trust and love. When has one of your relationships ended because of loss of trust? How did that trust get broken? In what relationships do you have trust? How would you describe what that feels like? And what does it mean for you to trust Jesus? What do you trust God for and about? Trust takes time and effort. "Trust is built with consistency" (Lincoln Chafee). Think over the following quotes about trust. Which resonate with you and why?

The best way to find out if you can trust somebody is to trust them.

—*Ernest Hemingway*

Trust is very hard if you don't know what you're trusting.

—*Marianne Williamson*

> *What loneliness is more lonely than distrust?*
>
> —*George Eliot*

> *Trusting is hard. Knowing who to trust, even harder.*
>
> —*Maria V. Snyder*

> *Learning to trust is one of life's most difficult tasks.*
>
> —*Isaac Watts*

Renew

Discipleship is relationship. When was the last time you thought about this basic premise of discipleship? One way we can define discipleship is "sustaining a relationship with Jesus." Relationships don't just happen, and they do not grow and deepen without our attention to them. How, in general, do you tend your relationship with Jesus? At the same time, we worry. We wonder, especially in the dark times of our lives, and especially during the COVID-19 pandemic, where is God? The woman at the well asked that question. Maybe her asking can help you ask, "God, where are you?" trusting that God will respond, "right here." In asking, the woman finds belonging. A kind of belonging she has never experienced. A kind of belonging that gives her a kind of connection, a kind of intimacy she has never known. A kind of belonging whereby she is deeply seen.

This kind of belonging actually changes who you are and who you think you can be—from useless to witness, from outcast to disciple, from left behind to deeply, truly, and abundantly loved. A kind of belonging that survives and thrives only because of trust. Because when you are seen, you can trust. To sense belonging, to know belonging, is to rest in mutual trust—the third key to unlocking your potential as a disciple of Jesus.

Prayer

Dear Jesus, oh how easy it is to allow our trust in you to wane. We get caught up in the "have tos" of faith, forgetting that what you want from us begins simply with who we are *with* you. Help us to lean fully into that trust—a trust that gives us the courage to ask the hard questions, to share our truth, and to see in ourselves what you already see. Amen.

Notes to Self

Chapter Four

Letting Go

In the end, she became more than what she expected. She became the journey, and like all journeys, she did not end, she just simply changed directions and kept going.

—r. m. drake

Focus Verses: John 4:25-30

[25]The woman said, "I know that the Messiah is coming, the one who is called the Christ. When he comes, he will teach everything to us." [26]Jesus said to her, "I Am—the one who speaks with you." [27]Just then, Jesus' disciples arrived and were shocked that he was talking with a woman. But no one asked, "What do you want?" or "Why are you talking with her?" [28]The woman put down her water jar and went into the city. She said to the people, [29]"Come and see a man who has told me everything I've done! Could this man be the Christ?" [30]They left the city and were on their way to see Jesus.

Read

Read the following passages in the Gospel of John. Note how they illustrate the five themes discussed in the *Introduction* (rebirth/new creation; identity of Jesus; relationship; witness; abundance) and the connections you are making to the *Focus Verses*.

John 1:35-51

John 6:20; 8:24, 28, 58; 13:19; 18:5, 7

John 6:35, 51; 8:12; 9:5; 10:7, 9, 11, 14; 11:25-26; 14:6; 15:1, 5

John 11:28-37

John 18:1-12

John 21

Review

Hearing Jesus's words about where and how to worship, the woman at the well makes another connection between what Jesus is telling her and who she knows her God to be, "I know that the Messiah is coming, the one who is called the Christ. When he comes, he will teach everything to us" (John 4:25; *Messiah* is the Hebrew; *Christ* is the Greek term). To what extent does she recognize in Jesus's words proclamations she has longed to hear, promises she has yearned to have spoken once again? The Samaritans had great expectations for a Messiah, especially to overthrow the rule of the Roman Empire and restore Palestine to its past glory. The hope for a coming Messiah is a thematic thread throughout all four of the Gospels—a hope rooted in God's faithfulness to deliver once again God's people from oppression. Just as God freed the Israelites from slavery in Egypt under Pharaoh; just as the Lord saw to it that their captivity by the Babylonians came to an end with a return to Palestine; so now Jews and Samaritans alike trust that God will free God's people from the tyranny of Roman rule. At the time of Jesus, Palestine was a Roman province, annexed by the Roman Empire, a colony, and thus, all inhabitants were colonized people. This hope for God's Messiah—the anointed one—to free them and rule as a kingly figure over Palestine was fervent.

One of the theological challenges for all the New Testament writers, however, was to reconcile Jesus as the Messiah with their inherited expectations of what the Messiah would look like and do. The assumption was that this Messiah would indeed reign over the kingdom, gloriously, like the kings of Israel before. Nowhere did the conceptions of a messiah include one that would be arrested, put on trial, and die. But not just die but be crucified—the most humiliating, shaming, excruciating death possible in the first century—a means of death adored by the Roman Empire because of its horrific and public nature. Crucifixion was meant as a deterrent. Those who thought they could stand up to Rome and get away with it only needed to see the crosses with dead and dying bodies lined up outside the gates of Jerusalem. Passing all those crosses as you entered the city was a reminder of what happens when you go against Rome—the empire strikes back.

In addition to the humiliating and horrifying nature of crucifixion, and that it was a Roman method of execution, was the devastation of crucifixion from a Jewish perspective. According to Jewish law, anyone who was hanged on a tree was considered cursed: "Now if someone is guilty of a capital crime, and they are executed, and you then hang them on a tree, you must not leave the body hanging on the tree but must bury it the same day because God's curse is on those who are hanged. Furthermore, you must not pollute the ground that the LORD your God is giving to you as an inheritance" (Deuteronomy 21:22-23). For Paul, reconciling this truth of God's law with how Jesus died is a topic of concern in his letter to the Galatians: "Christ redeemed us from the curse of the Law by becoming a curse for us—because it is written, *Everyone who is hung on a tree is cursed.* He redeemed us so that the blessing of Abraham would come to the Gentiles through Christ Jesus, and that we would receive the promise of the Spirit through faith" (Galatians 3:13-14). Making sense of the cross is inherent to the Christian faith, and what the cross means should not be a closed question in our lives of faith.

For all four of the Gospel authors, a central issue is understanding Jesus's ministry given their own expectations of what a Messiah would look like and what a Messiah would do. Each Gospel writer portrays Jesus in a different way, but they are all setting forth the argument that, indeed, Jesus is the longed-for Messiah. The question of whether characters in the Gospel narratives believe Jesus to be the Messiah is front and center—from John the Baptist (Matthew 11:2-6; Luke 7:18-23), to the disciples (Matthew 16:13-20; Mark 8:27-30; Luke 9:18-20), and now here in John, with the Samaritan woman at the well. For the Gospel of John, however, Jesus as the Messiah is not the primary christological portrait. As we have already seen, Jesus's identity is tied specifically to Jesus being God: "In the beginning was the Word, / and the Word was with God, / and the Word was God" (John 1:1). Jesus is the "one and only" God; the "begotten" God; this "unique" God, who reveals God: "No one has ever seen God. / God the only Son, / who is at the Father's side, / has made God known" (John 1:18). In the phrase "God the only Son," "only" can also be translated "one and only," "begotten," and "unique" from the Greek word *monogenēs*, a compound word from *monos* ("alone," "sole," or "only") and *ginomai* ("become" or "happen"). In our earliest and most reliable manuscripts of the Gospel of John, the word *Son* in the phrase "God the only Son" is not included in John 1:18. That is, it can read (and it is fun to compare translations here), "God the one and only," "the only begotten God," and "the only God." Later in chapter 3, Jesus will make this identification as God's only Son for himself: "God so loved the world that he gave his only Son, so that everyone who believes in him won't perish but will have eternal life" (John 3:16), and "Whoever believes in him isn't judged; whoever doesn't believe in him is already judged, because they don't believe in the name of God's only Son" (John 3:18). In 1:18, however, John makes an extraordinary claim: that Jesus is this unique, only, begotten God. This one-and-only God, who is at the breast of God, reveals God, declares God, and makes God known.

The woman at the well perceives in Jesus's words on true worship that he is "proclaiming all things" and states their shared hope in a Messiah. In this statement of hope, the woman at the well moves a step further in recognizing who Jesus is. In making the connection between Jesus's words and the promised Messiah, she goes beyond wondering if Jesus is a prophet to "could he be the Messiah?" Later in the passage, she will return to her town and wonder with them, "Could this man be the Christ?" (John 4:29). The fact that the Samaritan woman is this close to recognizing who Jesus is should truly give us pause. After all, she is not a disciple—or is she? The only other time Jesus is called "Messiah" in John is by one of Jesus's first disciples, Andrew, who "first found his own brother Simon and said to him, 'We have found the Messiah' (which is translated Christ)" (John 1:41). She is not a religious leader. She is not a Jew. She is not an insider. She is a woman. She is an outsider in every sense of the term, and yet here she is, staying with the conversation, sticking with Jesus this far. Even the disciples recognize this conversation as amazing when they return from town, "Just then, Jesus' disciples arrived and were shocked that he was talking with a woman. But no one asked, 'What do you want?' or 'Why are you talking with her?'" (John 4:27). At this point in the story, we should be on pins and needles, waiting for and wondering what will happen next. How will Jesus respond?

"I Am—the one who speaks with you." (John 4:26)

What happens next in this conversation is nothing short of extraordinary. To the Samaritan woman at the well, Jesus reveals his true identity. Jesus's response to her demonstrates that this has been a mutual, truth-telling, trusting kind of conversation: she shared her truth—"it's true, I don't have a husband"—and now, Jesus shares his, "I Am." This is what true relationship looks like and what Jesus desires with all of us. True relationship is mutual and reciprocal, not one-sided. All along Jesus has wanted the woman at the well to see who he really is, to know him. However, like she trusted Jesus with her truth, he has to trust her with his—and this is the moment.

Virtually every English translation of John 4:26 misses the mark by including the pronoun "he" after Jesus says, "I am." The NRSVue, for example, reads, "I am he, the one who is speaking to you." However, the pronoun "he" is not in the Greek text, and in fact, some Bibles will even note this by putting a superscript letter next to the "he" and then explain in an endnote, "not in the Greek text." It is an unfortunate decision on the part of translators to include "he" in Jesus's words because in doing so, we fail to notice the impact of Jesus's surprising and startling statement. Of all the English translations, the Common English Bible version above is one of few that comes close to capturing Jesus's revelation. Jesus clearly and directly says to the woman at the well, "I Am" (*egō eimi*). Ring a bell? That's right. This is God's response to Moses in the burning bush encounter: "But Moses said to God, 'If I come to the Israelites and say to them, "The God of your ancestors has sent me to you," and they ask me, "What is his name?" what shall I say to them?' God said to Moses, 'I AM WHO I AM.' He said further, 'Thus you shall say to the Israelites, 'I AM has sent me to you'" (Exodus 3:13-14 NRSVue). God goes on to tell Moses, "This is my name forever, / and this my title for all generations" (Exodus 3:15).

In this "I Am," Jesus reveals his true identity that we, as the readers of the Gospel, have known since the opening words of the Gospel. Jesus is God, the Word made flesh, the begotten God who now once again dwells with God's people (John 1:14, 18). This designation of Jesus as "I Am" is unique to John. There are two kinds of "I Am" statements in the Fourth Gospel. There are the "I Am" statements with a predicate nominative. A predicate nominative is a noun (or a pronoun) that renames the subject. In the Gospel of John, these are statements like "I am the good shepherd" or "I am the vine," (see 6:35, 51; 8:12; 9:5; 10:7, 9, 11, 14; 11:25-26; 14:6; 15:1, 5). The other kind of "I Am" statements in John are the absolute "I Am" statements—that is, those instances without a predicate nominative where Jesus simply responds with "I Am" (see 4:26; 6:20; 8:24, 28, 58;

13:19; 18:5, 7). Remarkable in the list of the absolute "I Am" statements in the Gospel of John is that the very first occurrence of "I Am" is for the Samaritan woman at the well—not for the disciples, not for the religious leaders, but for a religious outsider, for woman with no name, for the world (John 3:16). We are reminded of John 4:4, that it was necessary for Jesus to go through Samaria. Jesus had to go through Samaria to disclose to the world his true identity as the "I Am" in the world. Yet, Jesus's identity here is not just who he is but what being the "I Am" means. In Jesus's "I Am" to the woman at the well, we need to hear all of the "I Ams" of the Gospel. Jesus is her bread of life, her living water, her gate for safety, her Good Shepherd, her resurrection and life, her way and truth and life, her vine—the vine to which she now clings, to whom she belongs.

"the woman put down her water jar and went into the city" (John 4:28)

Leaving her water jar behind is a narrative detail often overlooked or explained away as unimportant. Remember, however, that details in Scripture matter and make a difference for what a story might mean. Imagine having to write on papyrus or parchment, trying to fit as many words as possible on each precious sheet. That was the situation for the authors of the New Testament. In fact, the earliest manuscripts we have of the New Testament are written in all capital letters with no punctuation or spaces between words. John did not have Microsoft Word to go back and edit. There were no typewriters with correction fluid like "Wite-Out." Whatever you include is a weighty decision. Why, John, did you deem it important to tell us that she left her water jar behind? I have many questions for John, assuming I will get to meet him someday, and this question is at the top of my list. Some commentators suggest that she left her water jug by the well because she was going to come back later to get it. Others argue that she was so excited, so eager to share about her encounter with Jesus, that she left it behind. Either interpretation may be valid, but neither is very compelling. And, with fetching water being one of her central jobs, a daily part of her existence and survival, leaving her jar at the well is a less than expedient choice.

Given the length of the conversation, the nature of the dialogue, and what Jesus has revealed about himself, could there be more to this detail? What might the water jug signify? Could it symbolize her shame? Her rejection? Her loneliness? Her guilt? Her dejection? Could it be that what she leaves at the well is the identity the world had placed upon her? Because she realizes, yet not fully perhaps, that she has a new identity? Not "five-time loser" but testifier? Not one to pity, but one to trust? Not "the barren one," but now the reborn one, a follower of Jesus? A disciple? Jesus found her and saw in her a witness. Maybe this is the moment she sees that about herself. But first, that means letting go. Letting go of what held her back and down. Letting go of the opinions of others. She is able to return to her town only because she leaves her water jar at the well.

"Come and see a man who has told me everything I've done!" (John 4:29)

The woman returns to her townspeople, but instead of making general statements about Jesus, she invites them to their own encounter with the "I Am." The words of her invitation are the exact same words that Jesus uses in his calling of the disciples. After John the Baptist points out Jesus to his disciples as Jesus walks by, saying, "Look, here is the Lamb of God!" the disciples then follow Jesus. When Jesus realizes that they are following him, he turns and says to them, "'What are you looking for?' They said, 'Rabbi (which is translated Teacher), where are you staying?' He replied, 'Come and see.' So they went and saw where he was staying, and they remained with him that day" (John 1:38-39). "Come and see" is the invitation to meet Jesus, to be in a relationship with Jesus. Invitation is the testimony of the ideal witness in the Gospel of John, one who has had an encounter with Jesus, learns who Jesus is, and then invites others to find out for themselves. In her invitation, the woman at the well is embodying the truth of John 3:16—for God so loves the world—as she herself has experienced this love. Later in the story, when the disciples try to get

Jesus to eat something (John 4:31), Jesus will urge his disciples to be like her, to witness as she did (John 4:34-38). The term "evangelism" or "to evangelize" (*euangelizō* is the verb form of the Greek word translated as "gospel" or "to share the good news") is never used in John. In our current times, the term *evangelism* often gets a bad rap. We have images of people knocking on our doors, with religious tracts, urging, "Are you saved?" trying to get us to believe their version of God. We have likely experienced conversations during which someone is out to convince us that their faith is the only faith, the only way. John sets forth a unique vision of what sharing our faith might look like, recasting our views of evangelism. Evangelism is witnessing and inviting, testifying and summoning. Her invitation to "come and see" also foreshadows Jesus's last meal with his disciples, breakfast on the beach. After the disciples haul in a net full of fish—153 large fish to be exact—he says to them, "Come and have breakfast" (John 21:12). "Come and see" leads to bounty and grace upon grace. "Come and see" is the summons of the Gospel of John—to see, taste, smell, hear, and touch your God in the flesh.

"Could this man be the Christ?" (John 4:29)

When the woman at the well says to her fellow village persons, "Could this be the Christ?" she is still wondering, asking the question of herself. In Greek, the syntax is such that her question expects a negative answer. A way to translate this construction might go something like this: "Surely, this is not the Messiah, right?" with the corresponding response being, "No, he can't be. There's no way." In this question, in this moment, we see that she is still not completely sure of Jesus's identity. We might want to cast a critical eye on her uncertainty—after all, the big reveal just happened. But that would be to diminish the truly remarkable revelation of Jesus to her—I Am. One doesn't walk away from an encounter with God having all of the answers. We might want to ask ourselves: would we be confident so quickly? Given the fact that her character is already suspect amongst her people, doesn't it make sense that she would hesitate in her convictions? Her lingering reservations capture the miracle of the moment—she has just met up with none other than the great "I Am." God—sitting on the stone brim of her well, tired and thirsty. She is awestruck and awe-filled. Persistent uncertainties seem appropriate.

Reflect, Respond, Renew

Reflect

When Jesus shares with the woman at the well his true identity as the eternal Word made flesh, the "I Am" standing right in front of her, I like to think that this is the original mic-drop moment. The woman at the well happens to mention a belief in, an expectation of, the Messiah? Jesus is all over that. I Am. God. Standing before you. Neither on this mountain, nor in Jerusalem. The last "I Am" statements Jesus makes in the Gospel take place at his arrest in the garden. He has been in the garden with his disciples, a familiar place for them (18:2) when Roman soldiers along with police sent by the chief priests arrive outside the garden to arrest him. Jesus comes out of the garden, leaving his disciples safely in the garden—the Good Shepherd keeps his sheep safely in the fold. He confronts the mob, giving himself up, and tells them exactly who he is (18:5). When the soldiers and police hear the "I Am," they step back and fall to the ground. Why? Because they are in the presence of God. This is a theophany, an appearance of God, and when that happens, you can't help but fall back. The Truth is right in front of you.

The conversation at the well is a mutual truth-telling encounter. How the world would be different, how the world would be changed if truth-telling were truly a pillar of our society. If we were committed to truth-telling and not lie circulating. If we were committed to truthful proclamation and calling out propaganda. If we were committed to telling the gospel truth and not the going-rate truth. To tell the honest truth and not tolerate hypocritical truth. To tell the factual truth and not believe fake truths, phony truths, and false truths that have nothing to do with truth and everything to do with power and control. Telling the truth breaks down barriers and exposes self-serving power. And in the end, truth-telling paves the way for authentic relationship.

Respond

Have you ever experienced that sense of awe when you think about God or think about being in the presence of God? Have you ever had an awe-filled moment before God? What is your response to imagining God revealing God's very self to you? "I Am. Right here in front of you. I Am right here when nobody else cares about you. I Am right here in your rejection, your hurt, your pain, your sense of unworthiness, your guilt, your humiliation, your shame, your indignity." The woman at the well is the first one to whom Jesus reveals who he truly is—the Word made flesh. It's a mutual truth-telling moment. She has told her truth. Jesus tells his. Sharing our truth takes courage, strength, and vulnerability. It means putting ourselves out there. Not everyone is worthy of our truth, and to some extent, people need to earn our truth. But when it comes to God, as much as we try to hide our truth, God sees us. What if instead of hiding from God, hoping that God doesn't see us for who we really are, we trust in God's love regardless of who we really are? That is what this story invites us to imagine.

Reflect

Jesus goes through Samaria because he needs a witness. And the woman at the well ends up being exactly the witness Jesus needs. She's the witness the disciples need to see. She's the witness that the people of Sychar need to hear. Jesus goes through Samaria not because of geographical necessity but for the sake of theological urgency. We tend to think that Jesus does all the work in our relationship. This story shows that what Jesus wants is reciprocity. And isn't that a hallmark of genuine relationship? Not quid pro quo, but a liberating mutuality. Jesus needs her witness. Witnessing to who God is for you is not about coercion, knocking on doors with pamphlets or threats. It is sharing your experience, your encounter with the living God, and saying "come and see." But it also means you will have to let go—of a lot. There is so much the prevents us from leaning into who God needs us and calls us to be.

Respond

Remember that the word evangelism or to evangelize does not appear in the Fourth Gospel. The Gospel of John frames testimony to what God has done for you as invitation. Perhaps you have wondered if part of being a good disciple is to bring others to faith. Can you imagine reframing your understanding of "evangelism" as invitation? It might help to remember that "evangelism" in Greek simply means "to share the good news." We share our relationship with Jesus or a special encounter with God not to force someone to believe in God or to have the same kind of faith as we do. Since God wants a relationship with people, they must have their own encounter with God and decide for themselves. We cannot make that decision for them, and we are not asked to judge them (John 3:17-21). The woman at the well must have been terrified to return to her townspeople and invite them to meet Jesus. I think we too are frightened to share what we know about God. This story encourages us to let go of our fears. What are we afraid of? Rejection, maybe, anticipating people to make fun of us, laugh at us. Or maybe we have other fears. Like, if someone else doesn't believe us, do we still believe in ourselves? When Jesus finds you, expect to be changed—maybe even to be reborn—into someone you never imagined. Who might that someone be? What would be your testimony about who God is, who Jesus is, in that case?

Reflect

"He cannot be the Messiah, can he?" expects a negative answer, something like, "Yep, you're right. No way is this guy Jesus the Christ." The woman at the well doesn't say, "For sure, certainly, absolutely, positively, no doubt about it, this is the Messiah." The question on her heart divulges that she does not have all the answers. The Samaritan woman is not totally sure that the man she met on her trip to the well was the Messiah for whom both she and her townspeople have been waiting. And yet, she does not allow her uncertainty to prevent her witness. Oftentimes, faith is cast as having the answers, especially when you meet people who do not believe in Jesus. You better have the right responses when the questions come up. We also do a lot of discipleship one-upmanship, and when we start thinking that way, no wonder we stay silent. But witnessing does not mean having all the answers or having all your theological ducks in a row. Remember, "faith" can also be translated as "trust." And we are talking about God, after all. When can we ever have all the answers about our Almighty God? Once we equate faith with knowledge or having the correct doctrine, it ceases to be faith. The woman at the well reminds us that faith means letting go of control and certainty. It means letting go of all judgment, competition, and expectation. As someone once said, don't compare yourself with others. No one can play your role better than you.

Respond

"The more certain you are the less room you make for faith" (Craig Barnes). If we expect to have God all figured out before going out and saying, "Come and see," well, it's going to be a long, long wait. If sharing your faith is not about having all the answers, do you think maybe you could tell others about what you believe? In the past, what has held you back from talking about your relationship with God? What have you been afraid of? What do you need to let go of? To leave behind? Maybe there's a time when you experienced rejection for what you believed. Maybe in the woman at the well, you can find some courage once again to tell others of God's love. Because, when God shows up—and don't worry, God will find you in your Sychar—when God reveals God's very self, God's true self, what will you do? I guess you could sit there. You could say, "Wow. Thanks. That's great. Would you like another glass of water?" Or you could do what the woman at the well does, which is likely why Jesus brought the disciples to Sychar in the first place. She shares her own experience, "He told me everything I have ever done," says, "come and see," and lets her neighbors decide for themselves. When we let go, this is the kind of witness I think we just might be able to do.

Reflect

Before the woman could return home to issue the invitation, walking that long dirt road back to those people who had no problem leaving her to fetch water on her own—those people who didn't want to be around her and those people who adjudicated her worth based on fake truths—she had to leave her water jar behind. She had to let go. In a lot of ways, she depended on that jar. It's what she has always known. As oppressive as it was, as demanding as it was, it's what she was used to. And more often than not, it seems easier to stick with the familiar than to lean into risk and change. More often than not, we continue to carry the burden, rather than imagine a life free of its weight.

A few years ago, I bought myself a journal. I am not much of a journaler, to be honest. I have tried over the years, from the teenage-girl diary, to special trips that I thought needed appropriate documentation and reflection. The journal was called "Letting Go—A Journal." I am still not entirely sure why I bought it at that time in my life. I have a few suspicions, of course. Maybe it was letting go of the mother I once had, who at the time was living in nursing care for Parkinson's. Maybe it was the process of moving my dad to a new apartment, watching him letting go of things that at one point in time had meaning, like deciding whether or not to keep his first-grade autograph book. "Dear Jack, it was fun when we made paper snowflakes." "Dear Jack, it was fun when we played on the playground together." Clearly, the first-grade teacher had coached the students on how to begin their entries. Maybe it was my divorce, knowing it was the best for both of us, but letting go of hopes and dreams. Maybe it was because that fall, I drove my oldest son out to Washington state for college. My son who came into the world nine weeks early at 3 pounds, 10 ounces. My son who was so very ready to discover what the world, what God, would hold for him. The Samaritan woman leaves that wooden bucket that has weighed her down far too long at the side of the well. She is no longer the person she has believed herself to be, or the person others had decided she was. Now she is the person God saw she was and could be. She is free.

Respond

What do you need to let go? What do you need to leave behind? What are your water jars? Those jars that give up and give in. That assume and accept. That disappoint and then determine a future without what you want and need in mind. What are those things that are weighing you down? That tell you that you are not worthy, that you are not enough. That prescribe how you should act and describe who you should be. What bucket will you leave at the well? When we can name those water jars and set them down, it is then that we might begin to imagine what God has in mind for us, what God might be calling us to do. Trusting in a future that God is fashioning, we are liberated.

Renew

When we hold on to ideals of discipleship, images of perfect faith, we forget that God doesn't see perfect—God sees good. So much of what we carry around about faith, like those water buckets, doesn't serve us. Do we believe what we are supposed to believe—according to what we were told by our family systems, our denominations, our churches? "The surest way to lose your self-worth is by trying to find it, through the eyes of others" (Becca Lee). This is true for faith as well. Might this be your moment to tell your truth about God because God knows your truth? Might this be a time for letting go of the "shoulds" and the "supposed tos," leaving them at the side of the well, and filling a new bucket with your thoughts and your ideas about God? Sometimes we even have to let go of our divine hold-ons—those perceptions of God that we thought couldn't or shouldn't change. Because of the COVID-19 pandemic, we've had to let go of a lot about church. What has been hard for you to let go? Richard Rohr says that "religion is one of the safest places to hide from God." The story of the women at the well reminds us that even God had to let go; God had to let go to become human. Letting go is a part and parcel of relationship and life. We let go of relationships that don't support us. We let go of scripts that could predetermine a new relationship. And letting go is the fourth key to unlock your potential as a disciple. We let go so that we can lean into what God has in store for us.

Prayer

Dear Jesus, help us to let go—of *all the things*. You know all the things because you see us. You know all the things because you know about us. You know everything we have ever done to try to be someone we are not. Those things that serve expectations and judgments. Those things that placate so as to please others, all the while forgetting that you seek us out in our Sychars. Thank you, Jesus, for going out of your way, literally, to find us. Amen.

Notes to Self

_____

_____

_____

_____

_____

_____

_____

Chapter Five

Witness

Like a wild flower, she spent her days, allowing herself to grow, not many knew
of her struggle but eventually all knew of her light.

—Nikki Rowe

Focus Verses: John 4:31-42

[31]In the meantime the disciples spoke to Jesus, saying, "Rabbi, eat." [32]Jesus said to them, "I have food to eat that you don't know about." [33]The disciples asked each other, "Has someone brought him food?" [34]Jesus said to them, "I am fed by doing the will of the one who sent me and by completing his work. [35]Don't you have a saying, 'Four more months and then it's time for harvest'? Look, I tell you: open your eyes and notice that the fields are already ripe for the harvest. [36]Those who harvest are receiving their pay and gathering fruit for eternal life so that those who sow and those who harvest can celebrate together. [37]This is a true saying, that one sows and another harvests. [38]I have sent you to harvest what you didn't work hard for; others worked hard, and you will share in their hard work."

[39]Many Samaritans in that city believed in Jesus because of the woman's word when she testified, "He told me everything I've ever done." [40]So when the Samaritans came to Jesus, they asked him to stay with them, and

he stayed there two days. [41]Many more believed because of his word, [42]and they said to the woman, "We no longer believe because of what you said, for we have heard for ourselves and know that this one is truly the savior of the world."

Read

Read the following passages in the Gospel of John. Note how they illustrate the five themes discussed in the *Introduction* (rebirth/new creation; identity of Jesus; relationship; witness; abundance) and the connections you are making to the *Focus Verses*.

John 11:1-44

John 14:1-14

John 15:1-17

John 16

John 17

Review

The Samaritan woman, transfixed and transformed, leaves her water jug at the well, heading back to town to tell and to testify. We know from 4:27 that the disciples have already returned to the well, having been in town to buy food. Verses 31-38 are frequently passed over when this passage comes up for preaching. I suspect that worship leaders, concerned with the length of this Gospel lesson, view these verses about farming and harvesting as an odd aside. What do sowing and reaping have to do with wells and water? The disciples are concerned for Jesus, "Rabbi, you need to eat!" Of course, we don't know how long it took them to go into the city for food. Jesus needs some nourishment before they get back on the road, and they've got a long way to go yet before stopping for the night. Jesus's response is rather puzzling, to say the least, "I have food to eat that you don't know about" (John 4:32). The disciples take Jesus literally, misunderstanding what Jesus is trying to say. I think, "Has someone brought him food?" probably went something like, "Did anybody bring him lunch? No, did you? I didn't. Not me." We saw the same kind of misunderstanding with Jesus and Nicodemus. Jesus said to Nicodemus that he had to be born again, which Nicodemus heard literally—"Wait, you want me to go back into my mother's womb and be born again?" Jesus offers the woman at the well living water, and she responds on a literal level, "Sir, you don't have a bucket, and have you looked down in that well? It's deep, all right." Like Nicodemus and the woman at the well, the disciples misunderstand Jesus's metaphor. But Jesus brought them through Samaria for a reason—for the disciples to understand what "God so loved the world" really means. The disciples themselves now have to move to the next level of understanding Jesus's mission—and their own.

"I am fed by doing the will of the one who sent me and by completing his work" (John 4:34)

To take the disciples to the next level of understanding of Jesus's identity, ministry, and mission, Jesus now spells out the symbol of food, just as he did with being born again/anew/from above, and for the woman at the well, the symbol of water. These elements—food, birth, and water—are certainly physical and real, but they have a symbolic meaning or a signifying function. That is, they stand for something else, pointing to a thing beyond what they initially appear to be. Often a symbol is a material object, like food in this case, that represents an abstraction. For John, these symbols direct us toward a truth that Jesus is revealing about himself. This symbolic meaning, however, can't replace the literal element. To do so would be to cast Jesus's ministry as only symbol and the Gospel of John will not let us assume Jesus to be mere metaphor. Jesus is the Word made flesh; we have to hold together both his full divinity and his full humanity. His body represents or points to God, but that doesn't mean his body, being human, is no longer important. In reading through the Gospel of

John, as soon as you want to choose one "Jesus" over the other—the human Jesus or the divine Jesus—the Fourth Evangelist reminds you that's not possible. For example, when Jesus hangs on the cross, an event he has seemingly orchestrated by giving himself up in the garden (there is no kiss from Judas) and carrying his own cross to the crucifixion site (there is no Simon of Cyrene to carry Jesus's crossbar for his crucifixion like in the Synoptic Gospels), he cries from the cross, "I am thirsty." This is the need of a very human Jesus. This is one of the seven of Jesus's last words from the cross and it is unique to the Gospel of John. Another example is the raising of Lazarus. While Jesus will raise a really dead Lazarus, Jesus weeps (John 11:35).

Jesus is not speaking of literal food but points the disciples toward a different understanding of nourishment. The food that Jesus provides is the very knowing of God. In his presence and ministry as the Word made flesh, Jesus makes God known—the nourishment we truly need: "No one has ever seen God. / God the only Son, / who is at the Father's side, / has made God known" (John 1:18). No one has ever seen God face to face, for to do so would mean death (Exodus 33:20; Judges 13:22); but in Jesus, our begotten God, we experience and encounter the fullness of God and God's grace upon grace (John 1:16). "Made known" can be translated as "reveal," "declare," or "make known," all of which have different meanings and connotations. "Made known" is probably closest to the essence of the verb, if we deem "to be known" as relational and not cognitive. Jesus comes not for us to understand God, but for us to get to know God, to be in relationship with God. The verb used here literally means "to bring God out." The idea is that through Jesus, God is now fully known and experienced, in a personal, intimate relationship, as close as it gets, resting on the very breast of God (John 1:18).

"Work" in the Gospel of John refers to bringing people to believe in God. In John 9, the disciples ask Jesus "who sinned?" when they encounter the man born blind. They voice the belief in the ancient world that if you had a physical impairment or ailment, it was the result of either your sin or that of your ancestors. Jesus nips that misconception in the bud. Basically, Jesus responds, "We will never know why this man was born blind. That's the wrong question. What's possible here is that God's works will be revealed with him!" (John 9:1-5). Indeed, the story ends with the blind man worshipping Jesus (John 9:38) and then Jesus explaining that the blind man is now one of Jesus's sheep because he heard and obeyed Jesus's voice (John 10:4). In the healing of the man born blind, Jesus has brought him into the fold of the Good Shepherd (John 10:16). Jesus's work is to bring God's love to the whole world, to bring sheep into his flock, and it is the job of the disciples to do the same: "I assure you that whoever believes in me will do the works that I do. They will do even greater works than these because I am going to the Father" (John 14:12). The disciples will do greater works than Jesus because the whole world is left to them once Jesus ascends to the Father (John 1:51; 3:13-14). The farming imagery communicates that the fields—that is, the world, which here the Samaritans represent—are ready for harvesting, inviting the whole world into relationship with God, with Jesus. It's as if Jesus is saying to his disciples, "Look around you, friends. Here is the world. See what the Samaritan woman just did? That's what I need you to do." Jesus brings his disciples to Samaria to show them, not just tell them, what their work needs to be. "Four months more then comes the harvest" communicates the urgency of this mission. This conversation is taking place just after Passover, in the spring, likely sometime in April. Four months from then would be the harvest time, but Jesus says to his disciples, "You cannot wait! The fields are ready! The time is now!" But, why the urgency? What's the big rush? The Word made flesh, the incarnation, has a time stamp. Jesus's time on earth, as the "one and only God," is limited. He will not be here, in this bodily form, to hear, to see, to smell, to taste, to touch—forever. To bring others into relationship with God through his presence as the "I Am" is "gathering fruit" (John 4:36) for eternal life. The life that Jesus offers—abundant life to its fullest (John 10:10) with him and with God forever—is available here and now. No waiting necessary. Eternal life is not only a future hope but also a present promise: "This is eternal life: to know you, the only true God, and Jesus Christ whom you sent" (John 17:3).

In verses 36-38, Jesus emphasizes that this work is a partnership between him and his disciples. The fullest expression of John 3:16 cannot be realized without the disciples sharing in Jesus's mission. Now it's the disciples' turn so that John 3:16 actually comes true. Jesus needs his disciples to realize, here and now, very early on in his ministry, that they will have to continue this ministry upon his return to the Father. The trip to Sychar brings the disciples' calling into full view. It was necessary indeed for them to go through Samaria.

"he stayed there two days" (John 4:40)

The Samaritans come to Jesus at the invitation of the woman at the well and then invite Jesus to stay with them, which he does, for two days. The verb translated "to stay" is used over forty times in John's Gospel. Our English translations render the Greek verb menō in several different ways—"to stay," "to remain," "to abide," "to dwell," even, "to continue" (John 8:31); but for each synonym it is the same verb. To abide with Jesus leads to relationship and denotes relationship. Abiding is John's preferred word to describe what a relationship with Jesus and with God feels like. And abiding is belonging. At the calling of the disciples, when Jesus turns and sees the disciples following him, he says to them, "What are you looking for?" Their answer, "Where are you staying?" is "where are you abiding?" At Jesus's words, "come and see," "They went and saw where he was staying, and they remained with him that day" (John 1:38-39). Both "staying" and "remaining" are the verb menō. When in the Farewell Discourse, chapters 13–17 of John's Gospel, Jesus says, "My Father's house has room to spare. If that weren't the case, would I have told you that I'm going to prepare a place for you?" (John 14:1-2), "room to spare" is literally "abiding places." You might have also read versions that have "dwelling places" or "mansions." The word is the noun form of menō and can also be translated as "rooms" or "abodes." Jesus will ascend to the Father (John 20:17), return to the Father, in order to welcome us into relationship with him and with the Father, again and forever. In John 15, Jesus continues to emphasize our relationship with him as "abiding" in the image of the vine and the branches, "I am the vine; you are the branches" (John 15:5). "Abiding" underscores the interconnectedness of the believer with Jesus. "Remain [abide] in me, and I will remain [abide] in you. A branch can't produce fruit by itself, but must remain [abide] in the vine" (John 15:4). This last "I Am" with a predicate nominative is the only instance where Jesus makes a claim about us as well—we are the branches. In doing so, Jesus emphasizes the abiding and belonging he wishes, for himself and for us. The vine cannot reach its full potential without the branches. The branches can't survive without the vine.

This abiding with Jesus leads to believing, or relationship with Jesus. For the Samaritans, many more believed because of abiding with Jesus (John 4:41). The verse, "We no longer believe because of what you said, for we have heard for ourselves" (John 4:42), is neither a slight against the witness of the woman at the well, nor does it discount her testimony, as some will argue. Rather, it is necessary to have your own encounter with Jesus, your own "born again" moment. You can't have a vicarious relationship. There's no such thing as a secondhand relationship. The Samaritans from Sychar abide with Jesus and believe for themselves.

"many more believed" (John 4:41)

The Samaritans believe because they have abided with Jesus. They have entered into a relationship with Jesus. In the Gospel of John, "believing" is a synonym for relationship. In fact, in the Fourth Gospel, "believing" is always a verb, never a noun; it is a state of being in relationship and not about a set of faith claims or religious convictions. Most of the time in the church when we talk about "believing" or "having faith," we mean holding fast to certain creeds or doctrines. These confessional statements or principles are often connected to our individual churches or to our denominations, like the Apostles' or Nicene creeds. For John, "believing" is not primarily about having the correct faith, although this Gospel does want you to recognize the truth of who Jesus is. To believe for the Gospel of John is to respond to Jesus's invitation, to come and see, and to trust in this relationship that leads to abundant life, both here and now, and in our resurrected life.

But what is this relationship, this abiding, like? Let's return to our discussion from the Introduction. Remember that in John 1:18, the last verse of the Prologue to John's Gospel, "at the Father's side" really means "at the bosom/breast of the Father." This intimate, personal relationship between Jesus and God was already stated in John 1:1, "the Word was with God." The Word has been and is with God, and now we are invited into this intimate, nurturing, life-giving relationship with Jesus and God. The kind of relationship that the Fourth Evangelist is trying to evoke is based on the kind of God imagined in this Gospel:

> But those who did welcome him,
>> those who believed in his name,
> he authorized to become God's children,
>> born not from blood
>> nor from human desire or passion,
>> but born from God. (John 1:12-13)

This parental image of God means that we are God's children, but not in a spiritual or euphemistic kind of way. John paints a portrait of our parent God who provides us with everything a child needs to survive and to thrive. As a result, the rest of the Gospel unpacks this parental image of God. A child needs water and food: Jesus is the living water (John 4) and Jesus is the bread of life (John 6). A child needs protection, to feel safe, and so Jesus is the gate for the sheep and the Good Shepherd who will not let his sheep be harmed by the thieves and bandits and wolves (John 10). And, a child needs nurturing, to have a sense of belonging. And so, Jesus offers the woman at the well a relationship she has never had before. She will be loved and cared for. She will be supported and encouraged. Jesus will be there for her, no matter what. Then, Jesus will find the man born blind after he has been cast out of his community for his defense of and confession about who Jesus is (John 9:34-35) and bring him into the fold of the Good Shepherd, giving him nourishment. Connection with Jesus is real.

For us also is the relationship that God and Jesus share. As discussed in the Introduction, the only other occurrence of the word breast/bosom in John's Gospel is when the Beloved Disciple shows up in chapter 13, "One of his disciples, the one whom Jesus loved, was at Jesus' side" (John 13:23). Most translations choose what they guess is a G-rated version of John and leave out "bosom." A more accurate translation would be, "Reclining at the table was one of his disciples, on the bosom of Jesus, the one whom Jesus loved." The setting is the foot washing, Jesus's last meal with his disciples, and the Farewell Discourse, that is, Jesus's parting words to his disciples before his arrest in the garden. It is a poignant scene, part of the same evening and string of events when Judas betrays Jesus and Peter denies him. Shortly after we meet the Beloved Disciple, Judas departs into the night (John 13:30). Jesus speaks what is known as the love commandment, "I give you a new commandment: Love each other. Just as I have loved you, so you also must love each other. This is how everyone will know that you are my disciples, when you love each other" (John 13:34-35), and then Jesus predicts Peter's denial: "Will you give up your life for me? I assure you that you will deny me three times before the rooster crows" (John 13:38). In the midst of betrayal and denial is the disciple whom Jesus loved, lying on the breast of Jesus.

But who is this disciple whom Jesus loved, the Beloved Disciple? If Jesus loves him so much, where has he been for twelve chapters? Commentators suggest a number of possible suspects—John the Baptist, John the author, Lazarus. But given that John's Gospel invites the listeners, the readers, into their own relationship with Jesus, I like to think that the Beloved Disciple is us—you and me. We are meant to imagine ourselves lying on the bosom of Jesus, just as Jesus rests on the bosom of God. I don't think it's an accident that the Beloved Disciple is never named. Neither is it an accident that the first time the Beloved Disciple is mentioned in John's Gospel is here, where two of Jesus's most intimate relationships—his friendships with Judas and Peter (John 15:15)—will be broken. Jesus will be abandoned, and so Jesus is comforted by this relationship with the Beloved Disciple, just when he needed it the most. Jesus needs us as much as we need Jesus because that is what relationship is all about. The next time the Beloved Disciple appears in the Gospel is at the foot of the cross. As he is dying, Jesus needs his mother and his friend to abide with him—and they do. They were the last ones he saw when he took his last breath. It is this kind of relationship that is envisioned every time we read the word believe. The Samaritans, the world, because of the invitation from the woman at the well, are now brought into the bosom of God.

"this one is truly the savior of the world" (John 4:42)

The Samaritans abide with Jesus and come to a remarkable conclusion: "we have heard for ourselves and know that this one is truly the savior of the world." Because of the witness and invitation of the woman at the well, the harvest is plentiful (John 4:35). This is the only time the term "savior" appears in the entire Gospel of John, and we hear it not on the lips of the disciples or people in the know, but from the mouths of the residents of a Samaritan city. What does it mean for the Samaritans to recognize Jesus as "savior of the world" when their only experience of Jesus has been abiding—and Jesus hasn't died yet? We are only in chapter 4. No arrest yet. No trial yet. No cross yet. Not even resurrection yet. With the exception of turning water into wine, Jesus hasn't done a darn thing, although that's a pretty awesome miracle, in my humble opinion. Salvation is supposed to come from Jesus's death on the cross, right? Salvation is the promise of our future resurrection, just as Jesus was resurrected, right? How is Jesus possibly the savior of the world here? In John 4:42? How is it possible that these Samaritans—and never the disciples—can call Jesus, savior?

For John, salvation is not from Jesus's death on the cross but is experienced in Jesus's life and ministry. Salvation, to be saved, is to have a relationship with Jesus, and with God—the closest of relationships where we experience abundant love and intimacy and belonging, reclining on the breast of God. The cross in John's understanding of Jesus's ministry is the inevitable outcome of what it means to be human—that is, we all die. The incarnation comes to an end at Jesus's crucifixion because it must—"it is completed/finished" (John 19:30). John understands salvation as already happening in the incarnation—the life and ministry of Jesus and thus, our relationship with Jesus. Salvation is certainly our promise after the grave (John 14:2), but we would overlook the fullness of this promise, the abundant grace upon grace love of God, if we didn't recognize that salvation is also ours here and now. Remember, even our future salvation is cast in these relational terms. In chapter 14, Jesus speaks about this promise to the trouble-hearted disciples: "Don't be troubled. Trust in God. Trust also in me. My Father's house has room to spare [abodes/dwelling places]. If that weren't the case, would I have told you that I'm going to prepare a place for you? When I go to prepare a place for you, I will return and take you to be with me so that where I am you will be too" (John 14:1-3). At the raising of Lazarus, even Martha does not understand this promise:

> Martha said to Jesus, "Lord, if you had been here, my brother wouldn't have died. Even now I know that whatever you ask God, God will give you." Jesus told her, "Your brother will rise again." Martha replied, "I know that he will rise in the resurrection on the last day." Jesus said to her, "I am the resurrection and the life. Whoever believes in me will live, even though they die. Everyone who lives and believes in me will never die. Do you believe this?" (John 11:21-26)

Martha believes in the resurrection—on the last day. But Jesus says to her, "yes and more. I am the resurrection and the life. Your life. Here and now. Lazarus's life. Here and now." To reinforce this promise, in the very next chapter we find Lazarus reclining on Jesus at the dinner table. Lazarus knows life with Jesus here and now.

Salvation as a promise for both future and present relationship is why the ascension plays such a critical role in the Gospel of John, even though it is never narrated in John as it is in Luke and Acts (Luke 24:50-53; Acts 1:6-11). While the resurrection is our hope of life after death, it is the ascension that makes it possible for Jesus to prepare abiding places for us to be with him and God forever. It is the ascension, not the resurrection, that is Jesus's culminating act of love, where he will draw all people to himself (John 12:32). In the garden, when the resurrected Jesus appears to Mary Magdalene, he doesn't tell her to announce his resurrection, "Christ is risen! He is risen, indeed! Alleluia!" Instead, Jesus asks Mary to proclaim his ascension, "Jesus told her, 'Don't hold on to me! I have not yet gone to the Father. But tell my disciples I am going to the one who is my Father and my God, as well as your Father and your God.'" (John 20:17). In the ascension, the Gospel comes full circle. In the beginning was the Word; and when the Word is resurrected, he returns to from whence he came. Notice that Mary also doesn't say, "Christ is ascending! He is ascending, indeed! Alleluia!" Rather she declares, "I have seen the Lord!" Mary Magdalene's expression is the Gospel in a nutshell—belonging. It is testimony that leads to, "Come and see."

Reflect, Respond, Renew

Reflect

There are many ways that we can define faith or think about what it means to believe in Jesus. The Greek word pistis can be translated "faith," "belief," or "trust." We most often construe faith/belief as something that we have or get. "Have faith!" Whenever I hear that phrase, my first thought is, "When did I not have it—and how do I get it back!" Faith becomes an achievement, of sorts; something to reach for. And it certainly doesn't include having questions. When you read or hear "faith," "belief," or "trust" in the Bible or in conversation, substitute one for the other and reflect on how that affects what faith means for you.

Respond

How have you typically defined faith? What difference does it make for you to think of belief as not a noun but as a verb? That to believe in Jesus is simply to be in relationship with Jesus, a relationship that has its ups and downs; that seems good and strong some days, and less so on other days, like all relationships. That belief is not something that you get from your efforts or sheer will; it's not an achievement with a gold star but is being connected to Jesus and to God, trusting daily in your relationship with Jesus. When we think of faith as relationship, we are far more forgiving of ourselves and of others. We don't put as much pressure on ourselves to have all the right answers about God. We simply lean on the breast of Jesus and trust.

Reflect

We sure spend a lot of time talking about salvation in the church. We worry if we are saved and exert a lot of energy worrying about whether others are saved. Rather than imagining how salvation might make a difference for our lives here and now, we've postponed its grace to our future. We've relegated salvation to a sort of get out of "you know where" free card. We think long and hard about who has it, if they should have it, all the while questioning, wondering, I sure hope I have it. As if salvation is something you accomplish, some sort of success, attained as a guarantee or as a reward for a life mostly well-lived. Salvation has even turned into a kind of religious competition. "How many souls have you saved?" It's become the ultimate hook for evangelism. People knocking on doors, standing on street corners, sitting behind booths in airports, asking, "Have you found Jesus? Are you saved?" But the story of the Samaritan woman at the well and the whole of the Gospel of John provide a different view of salvation. Salvation is not a feat of accomplishment or some sort of faith trophy. Salvation is reclining on the breast of God.

Respond

How have you usually defined "salvation," or what have you pictured salvation to be? Where did you learn the definition? How did that definition come about and what Bible passages were used to explain salvation? Have you ever thought about salvation as something that makes a difference for your life now, or has it always been equated with your future life with God? How might imagining salvation as relationship and connection with God, with Jesus, here and now, affect how you live your life? Would you live with less fear? Would you turn to God with trust more often?

Reflect

The woman at the well was "saved" that day—saved from shame and blame. Saved from guilt and pitying glances. Saved for a life with Jesus that led her to invite others to the relationship she had experienced in Jesus. Notice that she does not keep this salvation to herself. We tend to imagine salvation on an individual basis: "I am saved," or "Jesus is my personal Lord and Savior." But in the Gospel of John, Jesus came to save the world, embodied in the witness of the Samaritan woman at the well. Salvation has to be shared—not so that another soul is won for heaven, but so that God's love becomes how the world works. For the woman at the well, salvation means relationship with Jesus, and then reconnection with her community. The same is true for the man born blind; he is brought into the community that is Jesus's fold. Both were alone. Both were forsaken, neglected. Because of and through God's love, they are both saved for belonging. Salvation is belonging.

Respond

What will you do with salvation that's here and not just a life for which you wait or anticipate? Will you go to Sychar? Will you ask for that water? Will you tell your truth? Will you leave behind your water jar? Will you say, "come and see"? Because how can God love the world without your witness? "God so loved the world" is just about the best definition of salvation ever—to abide in God's love, a love that brings you into relationship with the entire world. A cosmic connectedness that can't be controlled by timetables or schedules, but spans the ages from the beginning.

Reflect

We do an awful lot of telling people about Jesus without actually inviting them into their own encounter with the living Christ. If witnessing to Jesus is just giving people information about Jesus, then just send out a mass email or a group text—a lot easier. Witnessing to Jesus is not the sharing of dogma, insisting on doctrine, handing out creeds and saying "believe." It's an invitation to salvation—not to be saved, but to your own intimate relationship with Jesus—here and now. Remember Mary Magdalene's testimony, "I have seen the Lord!" Because it's in that seeing and hearing and tasting and smelling and touching that salvation happens. John reminds us that we tell and then invite because others have to see it, experience it, for themselves. How are people going to experience the grace upon grace of God without a witness?

Respond

Can you be that witness, now that you have traveled with Jesus through Samaria? Can you be that witness when someone says to you, "I wish to see Jesus" (John 12:21)? Jesus brings his disciples to Sychar to show them that this is what "God loves the world" really means. It is a call to a kind of discipleship that takes courage, risk, and vulnerability. It might take you to places you don't want to go, encountering people you'd rather not meet, and maybe telling truths you'd rather not admit. It might mean trusting when it's the last thing you can imagine being able to do. You may have to give up things about your life on which you have always relied—control. Safety. Certainty. We want to hold on. Mary Magdalene certainly did. But she had to let go: "Don't hold on to me, for I haven't yet gone up to my Father. Go to my brothers and sisters and tell them, 'I'm going up to my Father and your Father, to my God and your God'" (John 20:17). What are you holding on to? Because if you let it go, you just might be born anew.

Renew

"The world is changed by your example not by your opinion" (Paulo Coelho). The fields are ripe for harvesting, not to win more souls for Jesus, but to invite others into God's love. When love reigns, when love wins, the world changes. That's all that witnessing is. It's simply saying, "I have seen the Lord! You gotta come check this out!" A witness can also be defined as "one who gives evidence." We say, "I have seen the Lord! Come and see!" not to prove God's existence, as if God needed our voucher. Instead, our witness confirms God is at work in the world, often for those who are having a hard time counting on that. When John writes, "Then Jesus did many other miraculous signs in his disciples' presence, signs that aren't recorded in this scroll. But these things are written so that you will believe that Jesus is the Christ, God's Son, and that believing, you will have life in his name" (John 20:30-31), "so that you will believe" is not singular; it's plural. Yes, we doubt God's trust in us. We doubt God's need for us. And so, the woman at the well, of all people, reminds us that Jesus went to Samaria with someone in mind—"can I get a witness?"—and that someone just might be you.

Prayer

Dear Jesus, help us to be the witnesses you need for the sake of the world you love. When you sense our uncertainties, our distrust and disbelief, pull us back to your loving breast to rest and be renewed, where we might belong once again. Amen.

Notes to Self

Epilogue

One day you will tell your story of how you've overcome what you are going through now, and it will become part of someone else's survival guide.

—Unknown

You belong. When we cast discipleship as being one whom Jesus loves, it changes the focus of the conversation. Discipleship becomes less about what we have to do. Instead, it flows from our state of belonging. Discipleship emanates from being found. Discipleship becomes first about what Jesus has offered you and not about how you can get Jesus to love you. It sounds different to say discipleship is being loved by Jesus, to belong with Jesus, than discipleship is being a follower of Jesus, doesn't it? Especially if following someone means blind adherence to principles. Following can sometimes imply that—an emotionless allegiance: "Don't think. Just follow!" In the calling of the disciples, Jesus first says "come and see" (John 1:39). Following happens after abiding (John 1:40, 43). John proposes that we think of following more like accompanying, because following leads to and embodies abundant life with Jesus: "I am the light of the world. Whoever follows me won't walk in darkness but will have the light of life" (John 8:12). When Jesus's sheep follow him, they know pasture and protection, sustenance and security: "Whenever he has gathered all of his sheep, he goes before them and they follow him, because they know his voice" (John 10:4; see also 10:27). But as we saw with the woman at the well, following Jesus, or accompanying Jesus, means letting go of the life you knew for the sake new life, new creation, with God. In Jesus's conversation with Peter on the Galilean seashore, Peter will have to let go of his concept of love and embrace God's love—a love that will take him to his own Sychar and his own cross:

> Jesus said to him, "Feed my sheep. I assure you that when you were younger you tied your own belt and walked around wherever you wanted. When you grow old, you will stretch out your hands and another will tie your belt and lead you where you don't want to go." He said this to show the kind of death by which Peter would glorify God. After saying this, Jesus said to Peter, "Follow me." (John 21:18-19; see also 13:36)

The keys to unlocking your potential as a disciple laid out—discomfort, wonder, trust, letting go, witness—are not a preset list of determined characteristics for being a faithful follower of Jesus; as if you can check them all off for an A-plus in discipleship. Instead, discomfort, wonder, trust, letting go, and witness all name what it's like to belong in a life-giving relationship. A life-giving relationship is one where there is deep mutual love, where reciprocity means both dependence and devotion, where trust gushes over; it is what salvation truly means. Through discomfort, God saves us from complacency. Through wonder, God saves us from rigidity. Through trust, God saves us from safe and calculated lives. Through letting go, God saves us from holding on to that which keeps us captive. And through witness, God saves us from ourselves—our inclination to keep what is meant for the world for our own personal gain.

The story of the Samaritan woman at the well might have us believe that one of these "keys" comes right after the other. That we can move through theses stages of relationship—discomfort, wonder, trust, letting go, and witness—in a linear fashion. That once we get to the last stage, witness, we have arrived! But these are not steps toward a goal. That's not how relationships work. We move in and out of these periods, these phases, depending on a lot of factors. Relationships are rarely stagnant. But when they are, you know you're in trouble. Imagine each key unlocks a door. You might remain in that room for a while, but the rooms are not necessarily adjoining.

We live in a weary world—a world still reeling from the trauma of a convergence of crises—COVID-19, the denial of racism and white supremacy, and our polarizing politics—that exposed just how much we were living with an illusion of control and an insistence on autonomy. And faith, the church, was no exception. We had gotten pretty good at monitoring faith, regulating faith, holding fast to a lot of churchy rules where the Spirit had little opportunity to blow as she willed or to birth anything. We became quite accomplished in minding our own believing business, our own congregational corporation, as if how we believed and how we did church didn't matter for God's world. If you feel like your faith, the church, even your church, is in a crisis mode, that's probably about right. Not "the sky is falling!" or "chicken little" syndrome or some sort of apocalyptic, Armageddon end times, but crisis as it means in John—a time of judgment and decision. A moment of judgment is not always a call to condemnation. A moment of judgment can be a moment of discernment, of decision. A moment for assessment and evaluation. For the woman at the well, it was a moment of response. These multiple pandemics created a merging of crises: societal, ecclesial (having to do with the church), theological, and individual. What kind of society systemically seeks to keep large numbers of persons enslaved? What is church now that God will not just be found in our buildings? Who is God and what is God up to when it seems like the world is falling apart? Where is God? And, who am I in all of this? Does God still see me even when I can't get to church? Is my faith still valid if now my Sunday mornings are spent watching the worship service on my sofa, in my living room, with a pot of coffee? Does Holy Communion still work if it's with a Ritz cracker and grapefruit juice?

Now is a time of crisis—a time to evaluate, discern, and decide. Can we live in the discomfort of Sychar, or will we sit around and long for life before the storm? Will we wonder about newness and possibility or wish for the normal we had constructed? Will we trust that the Spirit is breathing new life into dry bones once again or attempt to manipulate the rebirthing process? Are we willing to let go of what no longer gives life, or will we keep a white-knuckled grasp on what has died long ago? Are we willing to witness to the Jesus we know, or will we keep silent in the face of testimony bent on keeping Jesus from others?

The five keys to unlock your potential as a disciple—discomfort, wonder, trust, letting go, and witness—are not answers, but beginnings. We want to equate potential with capacity or capability, but that's not the only way to think of potential. Potential can mean budding, prospective, imaginable, possibility, and promise. The five keys are not orderly beliefs, but because you belong—to Jesus, to God—that's the promise. If Jesus can go to Sychar, Samaria, to find the woman at the well, Jesus will most certainly go wherever it takes to find you—the Beloved Disciple.

> *This is the disciple who testifies concerning these things and who wrote them down. We know that his testimony is true. Jesus did many other things as well. If all of them were recorded, I imagine the world itself wouldn't have enough room for the scrolls that would be written. (John 21:24-25)*